CW01496074

THE STRUCTURES OF EDUARDO TORROJA

THE STRUCTURES

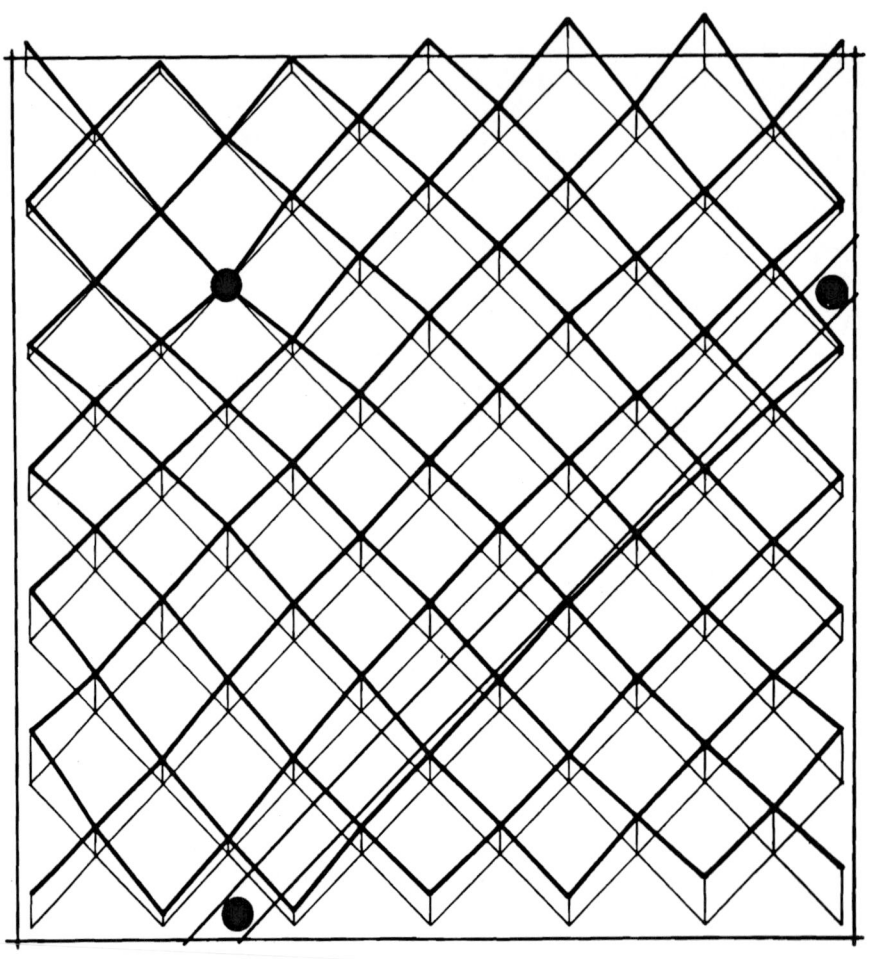

ЭF EDUARDO TORROJA

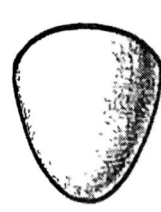

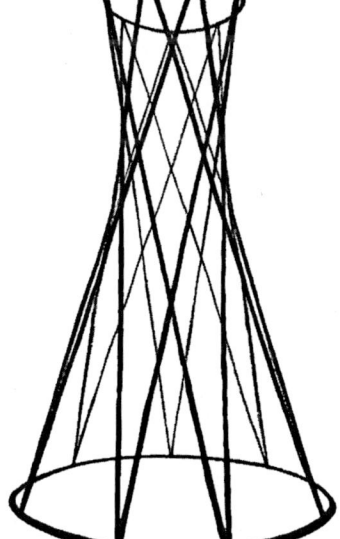

An autobiography of
engineering accomplishment

by Eduardo Torroja

Foreword by Mario Salvadori

F. W. Dodge Corporation, New York

© 1958 by F. W. DODGE CORPORATION

Printed and bound in U.S.A

All rights reserved

This book or any part thereof must not be reproduced in any form without the written permission of the publisher

Library of Congress Catalog Card No. 58-5170

In this book, for the first time, we have a comprehensive view of the remarkable career of Eduardo Torroja. Not only are the range and extent of his work fully represented, but Torroja himself has written the text and illumined the graphic presentation with his personal account of his design reasoning. And because Torroja is one of the world's truly great structural engineers, it offers lessons from which all of us can and should profit.

It is the dream of all serious students — a category that necessarily includes most practitioners — of structural engineering and architecture to work under an outstanding teacher in order to acquire that structural consciousness which is the only sound basis of design. Books on the theory of structures will give us some information on the mathematical analysis of certain standard structures, but it is only through a long period of apprenticeship that even unusual students learn the art of design.

First-rate professors of structures are, unfortunately, so rare that most of us are either left to our own devices or must undergo a painful period of unplanned in-service training. Too often, day-to-day work in an engineering office must be our substitute instructor in the basic elements of structural behavior.

Happily, a few great teachers in the field of structures are willing to impart their patiently acquired wisdom to anyone who can study their published works. One of them is Eduardo Torroja y Miret, and the tersely annotated pictorial summary of his career which he presents in these pages is the most concentrated of all textbooks.

Eduardo Torroja is, of course, much more than a great teacher of structures. He is a humanist, a wise administrator of large enterprises, a great engineer, and a zealous researcher.

It might be well to point out to the hurried reader and the impatient student that no man becomes all these things overnight or by being born "lucky." The curve followed by Eduardo Torroja in becoming such a complex personality is the curve followed by most men who reach such high levels. They usually devote their beginning years to a long and thorough study of the fundamentals of their culture. To this discipline Torroja added a deep understanding of the humanities and of mathematics.

v

In their second phase of development, such men apply the fundamentals they have mastered to the solution of original problems, thus acquiring powerful techniques for the enlargement of their scope beyond its original limits. The third phase starts when the experience accumulated in the second is slowly synthesized and becomes what we call "intuition." Their brains then perform the most complicated evaluations and calculations so rapidly that the essentially rational character of the process is masked by its swiftness.

The last phase, which never ends, brings them to higher and higher levels, with ever-decreasing effort and ever-increasing enjoyment of their work. It is in this final phase that they necessarily become teachers, whether in or out of a school.

Torroja is an outstanding example of the exceptional structural engineer. Mathematically minded, and aided by the extraordinary physical intuition with which his creative growth has endowed him, he designs his structures on the sound bases of economy and strength. But the humanist in him has a flair for the beautiful, and a refined, delicate sense of beauty pervades his conceptions in space. So subtle is his esthetic feeling that you will find him spacing a set of columns at different intervals in order to achieve a pleasing architectural rhythm, thus repeating in concrete what the Greeks did in marble. Or you will find him boldly contrasting color with the delicate grey surfaces of his concrete.

And the concrete itself is delicate and perfect because his aggregates have been chosen on scientific grounds in the Technical Institute of Construction and Cement at Costillares, which he himself created and has directed since its foundation. Few of his structures indicate his many-faceted intelligence more clearly than the buildings of this institute, in which audacious polygonal forms are mixed with delicate curves, and shells lean on folded plates. And, lest the visitor should miss the point, Torroja is eager to have him notice that the curved frames supporting the lovely pergola he is walking under are Bernoullian lemniscates.

The Costillares institute has one of the world's three outstanding model testing laboratories, and the results of its tests are the basis for most of Torroja's own complicated designs. Torroja, the engineer, is steeped in theory, but he knows when one must stop believing blindly in mathematical derivations and resort to experimental stress analysis.

One striking feature common to all the structures so brilliantly discussed and lucidly explained in this book is their lack of frills. We must realize that Torroja works in and for a country in which esthetic values have always had tremendous importance for the individual and the race, but in which lack of wealth makes it impossible, even today, to improve the appearance of a building by decorative additions. This is, perhaps, a blessing in disguise, since the essential serenity and beauty of Torroja's structures is often the byproduct of a limited budget. As has so often been true in the history of creative achievement, the limitations themselves — the very factors interfering with the solution of a problem — enhance the intrinsic value of the final product.

A preface can never do justice to a book. Here in a few pages is a parade of works conceived and built over a period of 32 years by one of the great engineers of our time. He has chosen only 30 structures out of the hundreds he has designed and built. But they cover a great variety of situations: from a subway station in concrete to a church in brick, from a bridge to a dam, from a hangar to a restaurant. And many of the brief discussions allow us to follow the creative process of the designer even when this process originally occurred in rapid flashes of insight. We can also appreciate the innumerable difficulties he conquered, the subtle reasons for his choice of forms and practical solutions, and his familiarity with the behavior of materials as different as steel and brick.

Torroja was a pioneer in 1933 and is a leader in design today. As a personal friend of this extraordinary engineer, I felt privileged to peruse his book, where he stands revealed in a new perspective. The designer and the artist are displayed by his works, but here we can see the humor and wisdom of the man himself.

Mario Salvadori

CONTENTS

This work is now ready for the printer, and the editor has asked me to provide a preface. An awkward task, this, to write an introduction to a mere series of descriptive sketches of some of my works. All I can say is that in each of these projects I have tried to understand as completely as possible all the factors involved and to apply my ingenuity to achieve a satisfactory solution, both structurally and economically. My final aim has always been for the functional, structural, and aesthetic aspects of a project to present an integrated whole, both in essence and appearance.

Many of my works are not mentioned here, but I feel that the few which are included best exemplify what I was searching for, and what I finally achieved.

And now it is for the reader to judge them. If he discovers anything useful in the following pages, I will be glad to offer it to him, and if there is anything to criticize, I hope he will do so freely.

The author takes pleasure in citing the architects, engineers, artists, and contractors with whom he worked jointly in the following projects·

MADRID RACECOURSE
Architects· C Arniches, L Dominguez
Contractor Agroman

MARKET AT ALGECIRAS
Contractor R. Barredo

FRONTON RECOLETOS
Architect S Zuazo
Contractor: F. Huarte

TACHIRA CLUB
Architect F Vivas

TEMPUL AQUEDUCT
Contractor Hidrocivil

QUINCE OJOS VIADUCT
Architects· M L Otero, A. Aguirre
Contractor· Agroman

ALLOZ AQUEDUCT
Contractor: F. Huarte

ESLA ARCH
Engineers: C Villalba; A Salazar
Contractor: OMES, R. Barredo

SKEW SLAB BRIDGE
Engineer. A. Páez

COSTILLARES BUILDING
Architects: G Echegaray, M Barbero

CANELLES DAM
Engineer: C Benito

WATER TANKS
Engineers· A Páez; F del Pozo
Contractor: F. Fernández

HANGARS
Contractor· OMES

TRIANGULATED SHELL ROOF
Engineer· F del Pozo
Contractor· OMES

LAS CORTS FOOTBALL STADIUM
Architect. J M. Sagnier
Contractor· J Pujadas Jorba

COMPOSITE BRIDGES
Engineer: G Andreu
Contractor· OMES

PONT DE SUERT AND XERRALLO
   CHURCHES
Architect J. R Mijares
Paintings· M Roesset
Sculptures J. Higueras

PHOTOGRAPHS
M Garcia Moya

DRAWINGS
G Echegaray

1 LARGE SHELLS

I have often been asked how I came to decide upon the design of the Zarzuela Hippodrome, and as this book now affords me an opportunity to do so, I will try to explain it here.

The functional requirements may be ascertained from the cross section below, namely: Spectator stands with a clear view of the race track; a promenade at the top of the stands to face the track on one side and the paddock on the other; a betting hall opening onto the paddock; a double row of betting offices facing the betting hall on one side, and on the other, the gallery leading to the stands and track; a second promenade at track level with more betting offices; a staff gangway; and finally, the roof over both the top promenade and the public stands.

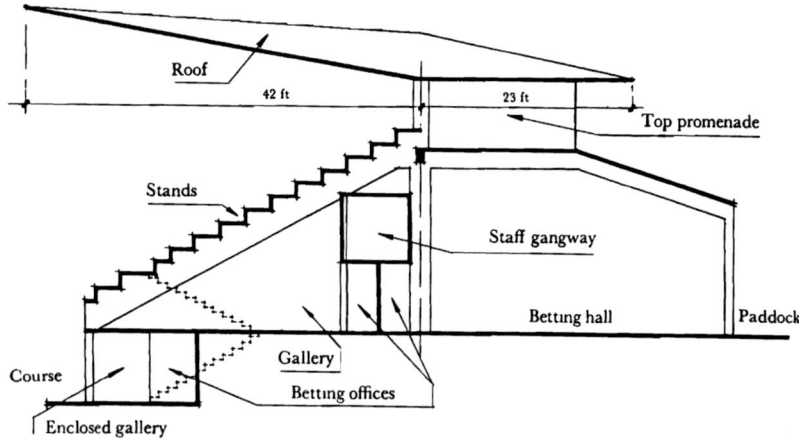

Quite obviously the first pattern (that of the cross section) was not very satisfactory. Without going into details, it is clear that the weight of the cantilevered roof over the stands will be greater than the counterweight over the top promenade. As the rear support will consequently be in tension, it has to be a tie rather than a strut. On the other hand, the other support has to take the whole weight of the roof plus the additional load applied by the tie member. Thus this support must serve as the main and most massive one, and the rear support need only be a rod.

The weight of the roof over the betting hall will be largely offset by the tie member, and the load on the columns supporting the betting hall roof on the paddock side will be slight. Therefore these columns can be omitted in order to improve circulation with the exterior as well as provide continuity with the surrounding open space.

To employ a second column close to the main one for the support of the gangway would be both awkward and strange. As the main support has to be massive, there will be no difficulty in supporting the gangway on a structure cantilevered from it.

On the race track side, supports along the bottom edge of the stands are also unnecessary because the height between the track and the underside of the stands is sufficient to accommodate a cantilevered beam.

Thus the initial plan developed into the one shown in the sketch below. On close inspection, it becomes clear that the depth of the roof structure will increase from the free edge to the point over the main support and then decrease towards the tie member. A rigid attachment at the main support is not very useful, because the roof has good stability under the dual vertical forces provided by the main support and tie. On the other hand, it is essential—particularly as a safeguard against wind forces—that the main support be rigidly fixed at the promenade level.

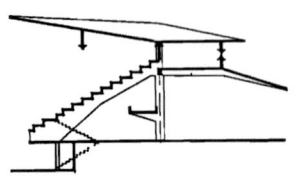

FIRST REVISION

VIEW FROM PADDOCK DURING CONSTRUCTION

The cantilever roof of the betting hall must be flat over the top central portion, to provide a floor for the top promenade, whereas the rest of it should slope downwards, to pose as little interference as possible with the views of the paddock from the promenade. Furthermore, the depth of the cantilever has to increase towards the main support, where bending moments are highest.

The main support, in turn, must resist these moments. Its full section could be extended to and fixed rigidly in the foundation in order to resist wind forces. However, the inclined construction supporting the main stands provides a better means of achieving lateral stability. Horizontal forces can be taken along this sloping beam to the other ground support more efficiently and more economically.

In such a structure, the existence of two very rigid supports (the main one plus the bottom part of the stands) could restrain too severely the thermal expansion or shrinkage of the portal frame (which consists of these two supports and the connecting slope of the stands). Hence it seemed advisable to reduce the over-all rigidity of the main support without impairing its capacity to transmit horizontal shear to the promenade level. The provision of a flexible joint at the bottom of the support consequently seemed a natural, if not an essential, step.

Finally, the scant height between the staff gangway and the structure supporting the stands made it necessary to reduce as much as possible the depth of the latter structure over the gangway.

At this point, the design shown in the top sketch at the left was allowed to rest for a while, in order to free the imagination and give it a better chance to refine the ideas further into a clear, well integrated whole. In the end, the design was given a certain curvature of outline, as illustrated in the bottom sketch. This seemed so straightforward and suitable to the purpose that the imagination resisted any new attempt at further improvement.

After having adopted curved outlines for the lower part of the structure, it seemed reasonable to give a curved form to the roof also. To make this a flat slab supported by strong ribs hidden above it seemed a heavy and unaesthetic solution. For a longitudinal row of columns, the most obvious choice would be a series of vaults from support to support, as shown on page 7.

More was involved, however, than the mere running of an arch or vault from one support to the next. The main structural function of such vaults is that of arched cantilevers. And to meet the strength requirements of such cantilevers it is necessary that the height-span ratio of the vaults be greatest over the main supports and decrease

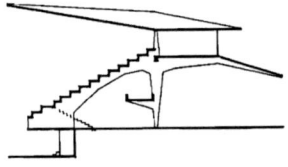

SECOND REVISION

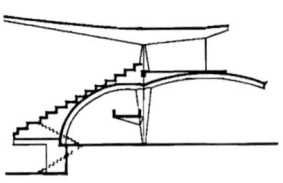

FINAL REVISION

SHELL ALTERNATIVES: ARCADE

towards the free edges. Of the many basic types, the resulting surface could well have been a conoid but for the objection that the conoid is not very attractive. It seemed preferable to choose some other form of curvature. Among the better known ones, none seemed more adaptable than the hyperboloid; hence these cantilevered vaults have the shape of hyperboloidal sectors.

And the question now arises: Is the invention of an especially adapted form to solve a specific problem strictly an imaginative process, or is it the result of logical reasoning based on technical training? I do not think it is either of the two, but rather both together. The imagination alone could not have reached such a design unaided by reason, nor could a process of deduction, advancing by successive cycles of refinement, have been so logical and determinate as to lead inevitably to it—whatever the reader of these lines may have inferred.

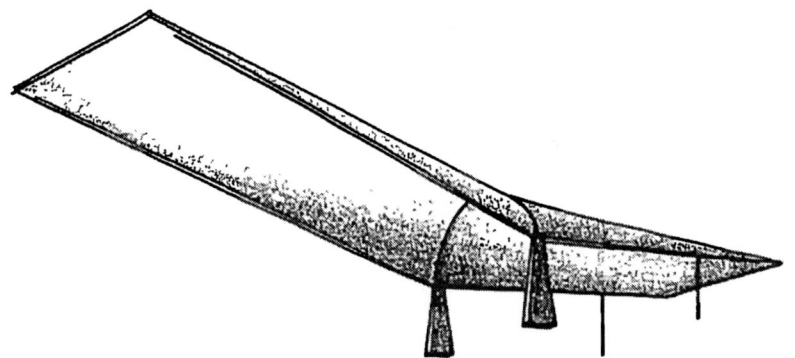

SHELL ALTERNATIVES CONOID

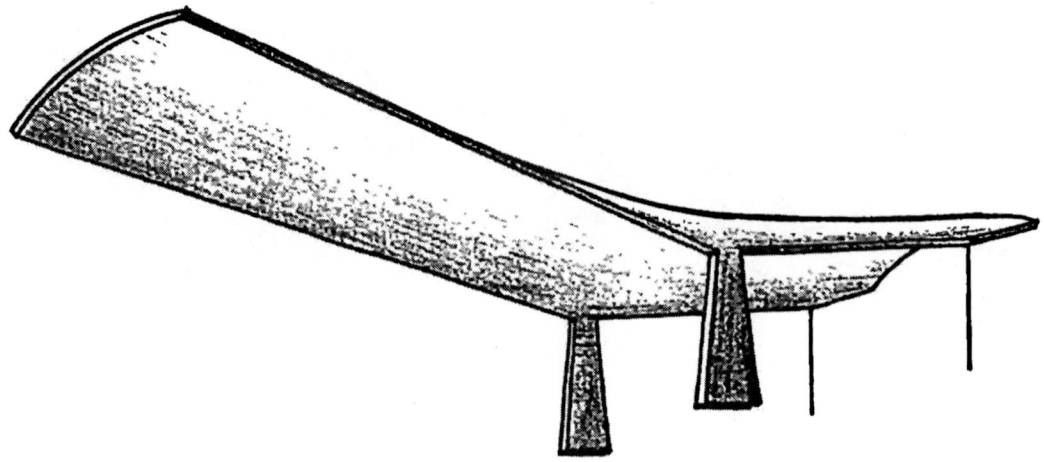

SHELL ALTERNATIVES· HYPERBOLOID

This design was intended for a competition that had a three-months time limit. A considerable proportion of this time had to be spent in working out preliminary functional problems. But the truth is that the whole process just described was a matter of a few minutes (possibly seconds), and that these ideas and final form became evident all at once, unexpectedly, at one o'clock in the morning, with only a few days left before the expiration of the final date for submitting the designs and when it seemed certain that we had lost all chance of winning the competition.

Each person can make his own inference, but it would not be amiss to meditate on the above phenomenon. To me it seems clear that the imagination can operate successfully only in conjunction with the basic principles that a long experience of technical creative work leaves in the unfathomable depths of our personality, so that these may later subconsciously condition our own intuitive thought. But those basic principles are not enough in themselves to create, critically and deductively, a new form. For this to emerge, a spark of imagination is required. Indeed, it often appears at the most unexpected moment, when we are least trying to create.

But let us leave aside these speculations—certainly not original to those who occupy themselves with such matters—and return to the work under discussion. I had mentioned that the roof finally selected consists of overhanging hyperboloidal sectors. These are 42 ft long. Over the main supports each lobe has a rise of 4 ft 6 in., and a radius of curvature of 9 ft, whereas at the free edge the rise of the arch is reduced to 1 ft 7 in., the radius of curvature increases to 22 ft, and the thickness is 2 in. With these proportions, the sense of lightness intrinsic in this type of shell is particularly emphasized.

The mutual intersection of these hyperboloidal sectors would result in a curve with its convexity downwards, as shown below (Fig. A). Such a profile would have the advantage of showing more clearly that these vaults, so far from being supported by the lower-chord cantilevered beams (hidden above the vaults), are themselves the real supporting structure, and that in actual fact, the lower edges hang from the rest of the construction, whereas the crowns weigh down upon the whole. In each vault the haunches may be regarded as the web of a beam in which the crown of the vaults corresponds to the tension chord, and the edges along which the vaults meet each other to the compression chord.

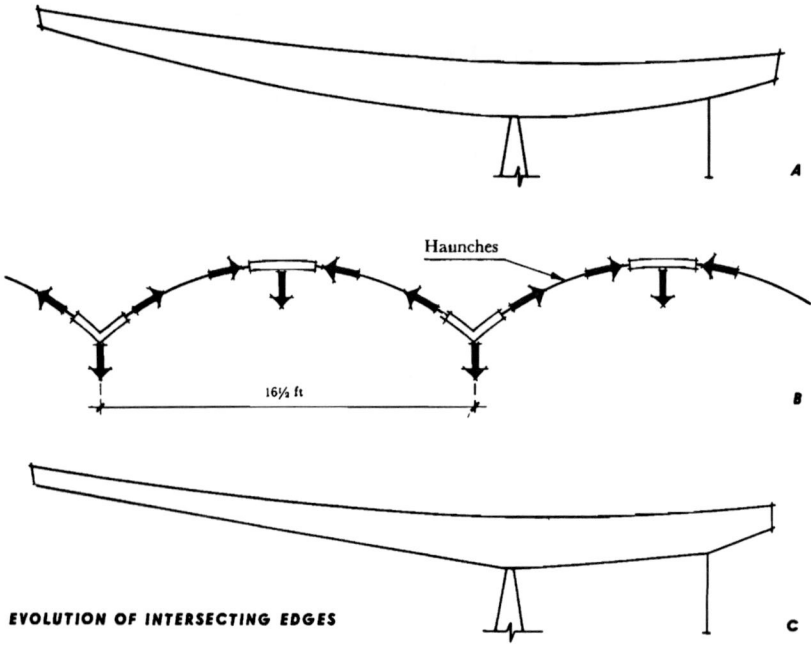

EVOLUTION OF INTERSECTING EDGES

PROMENADE SUPPORTS

Naturally, it is an oversimplification to identify the structural pattern of these lobes with that of the simplest type of beam, that is, with two well differentiated chords connected by an intermediate web. In reality, the phenomenon is both more complicated and more simple. The clearest description of it is provided, as always, by a pattern of isostatic lines. The particular pattern here is a family of arcs in compression kept in equilibrium by an orthogonal family of cables in tension, the whole assembly being linked together in space along a surface of double curvature (see following page). Each element of the shell weighs directly on this double family of stressed members, which then transfer these forces (the elementary weights) to the roof supports.

This structural pattern is not typical of hyperboloidal surfaces only; it applies equally to any cantilevered curved surface.

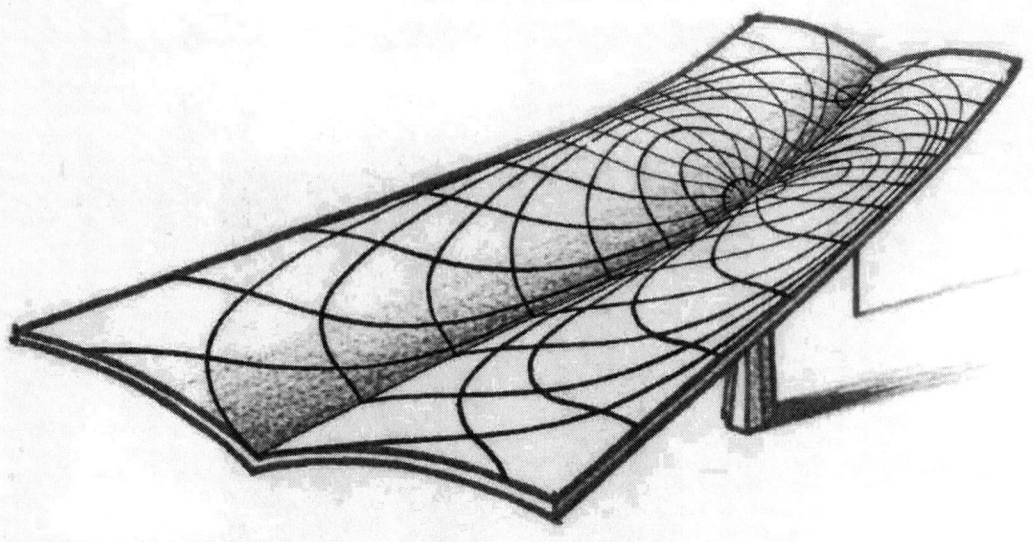

DISTRIBUTION OF STRESSES

Hence there was no need to adopt this standard surface precisely, and it was thought preferable to modify it slightly. The possibility of making the lines of intersection curve downwards had been contemplated, but finally this shape was discarded, and it was decided to have straight lines of intersection sloping up towards the free edge (Fig. C). It was felt that lines of intersection curving downwards would be less agreeable to the eye, or would at least be too startling to observers accustomed to a more classical expression. The curved part of the shell, however, was to retain the general shape of a hyperboloid.

The theory of elasticity has not yet developed a suitable mathematical technique for a stress analysis of this type of structure. However, even without precise analysis, it is known that they possess good structural properties in space. For the present building, a number of trials were undertaken with the sole purpose of obtaining an idea of the direction and intensity of the probable stresses (see diagram above).

The problem became particularly complicated because of the relatively strong reinforcement (see opposite page) that runs through the most highly stressed part of the structure—at the crown of the vault near the main supports, where the curvature is greatest. The radial components of the tensile loads in these curved rods—which are resisted by the concrete in a plane tangential to the lamina—are internal forces that have to be considered in studying the equilibrium of the central part of the lobes. But these are technical minutiae that extend beyond the scope of this text.

It was finally decided that it would be best to construct a model, and the contractor offered to make a full-scale one, that is to say, to build a finished lobe for experimental purposes (shown above). This operation was also to serve as a check on the construction procedure. The same formwork could be used for ten other lobes (the whole project necessitated the use of only three different forms) and the reinforcement totally recovered, because the lamina was so thin that it was easy to remove the concrete without damaging the steel. Hence this experimental lobe involved the loss of only 424 cu ft of concrete, which was the full volume of the whole lobe.

UNIT UNDER FULL LOAD

On being tested, the model proved to be three times stronger than was necessary to meet normal loading conditions, including its own weight and snow overload.

As an indication of their strength, it might be of interest to mention that these stands were close to the battle line for several months during the Spanish Civil War and were subjected to several bombardments. As a consequence, the roof was hit and perforated 26 times and the shell repeatedly cracked by the strong vibrations sustained. In spite of this abuse, the roof withstood the damage very well. It is still in very good shape, for the holes have been concreted and stiffeners added to the tips of the end lobes. These had drooped slightly because of the explosions, giving the stands a bedraggled air.

Structural details are of comparatively little interest in a description of this kind. In brief, the thickness of the shell varies from 2 in. at the free edge to 5.5 in. at the crown of the vaults over the main supports. The concrete joints occur along the crown of the lobes where the danger of water seepage through the joints is least. Only thin transverse reinforcing rods run across these joints. The lower vaults are 2 in. thick throughout their whole surface. The lightness and curvature

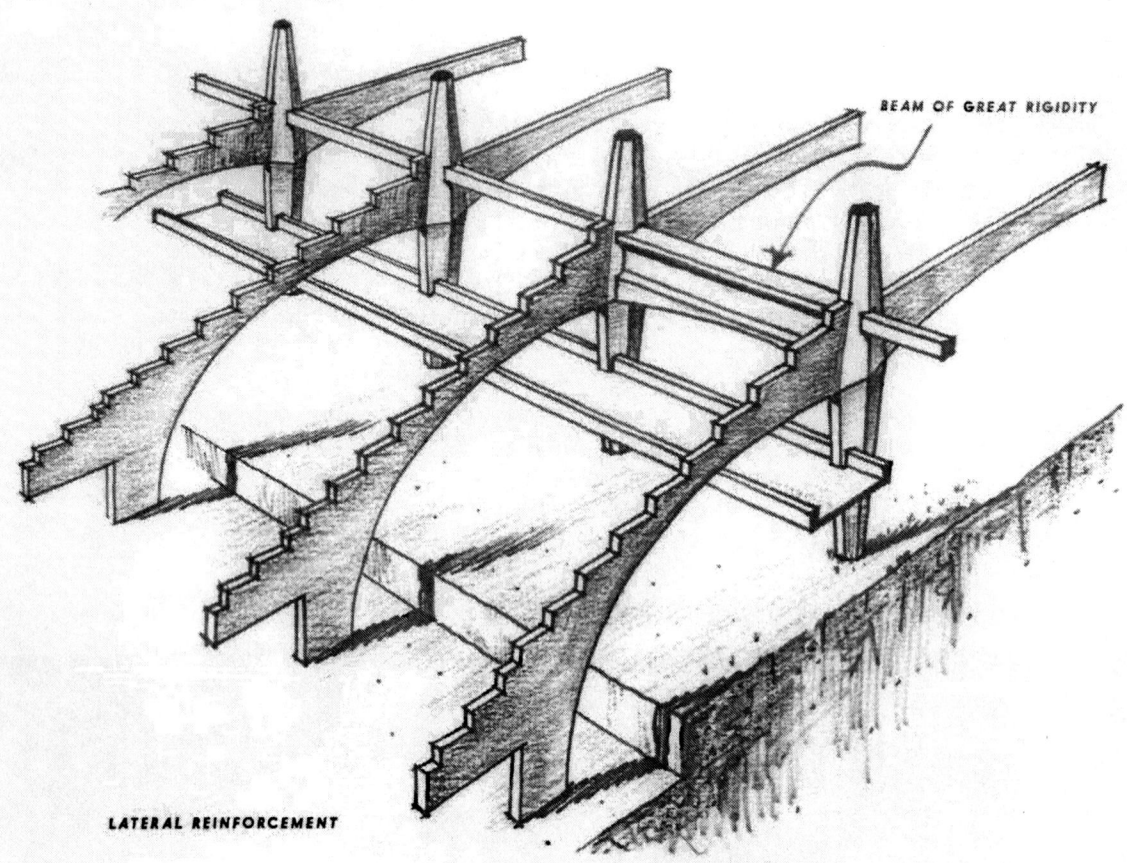

BEAM OF GREAT RIGIDITY

LATERAL REINFORCEMENT

of these shells facilitates their expansion under temperature changes. But for the same reason, they do not provide adequate bracing for the transverse portal frames, which are spaced at 16-ft intervals. For lateral stability, therefore, a longitudinal beam is provided that forms a stiff portal frame in conjunction with the middle transverse frames supporting the public stands. On either side of these two central frames, the longitudinal beam is continued in the same plane but in a much less rigid form, so as to connect all the other transverse frames to the central ones. Its low rigidity facilitates longitudinal thermal deformations, which are finally transmitted to the terminal frames. These are sufficiently flexible to adapt themselves to the change in length of the longitudinal beam.

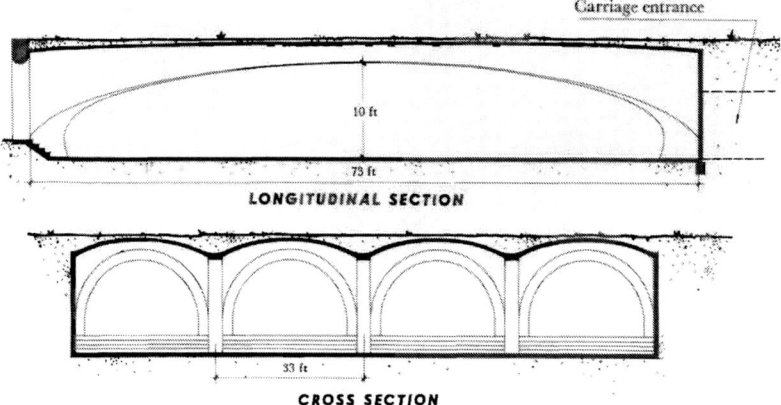

Carriage entrance

10 ft

73 ft

LONGITUDINAL SECTION

33 ft

CROSS SECTION

The structure just described seeks to convey the maximum sense of spaciousness in the lower floor level. It relates harmoniously the volumes of the large betting hall and the gallery beneath the stands so that these appear to be continuous across the suspended gangway and the betting offices (which could have been made practically transparent by the use of glass screens).

On the side of the track, the roof of the lower gallery consists of the overhanging stands structure, so that the arcade which appears to support the lower part of the stands is false. It was added later in search of effects and for other reasons that are unrelated to the basic purpose of the design.

The underground hall providing access for vehicles to the presidential stand is an almost independent aspect of this project. In spite of the low headroom available, it was possible to build a number of double-curvature vaults, as shown above. Over these vaults an earth fill serves as a platform for an open-air restaurant.

The double-curvature vaults are circular in one vertical plane, and elliptical in a plane normal to the first.

STAIRS LEADING TO STANDS

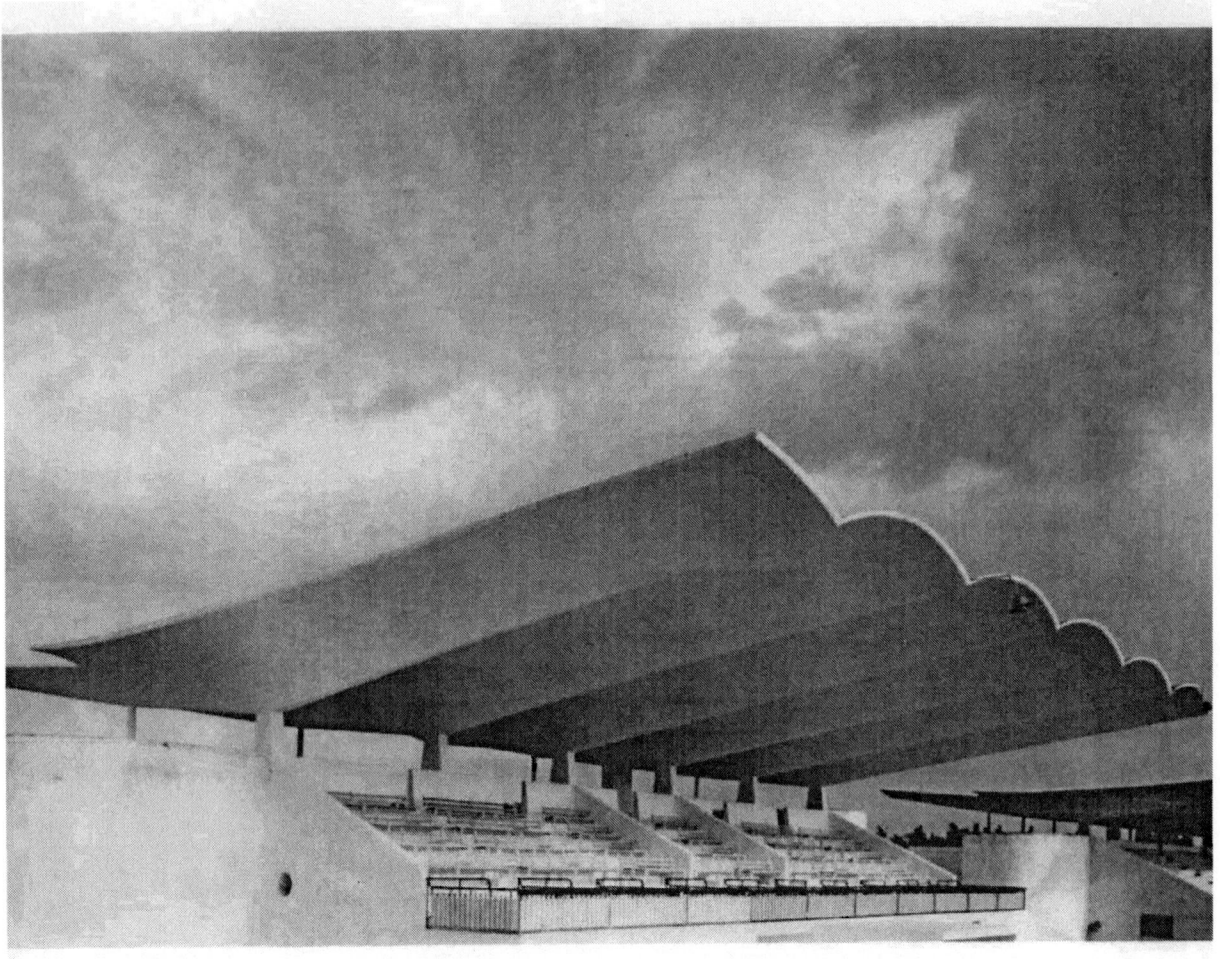

The very low height-to-span ratio of the elliptical arches (a height of 10 ft at the crown for a 73-ft span) made it necessary to link together the abutments by means of tie rods placed under the flooring. Even so, the elastic stretching of these rods might have induced undesirable bending moments at the crown. This danger was avoided simply by providing the tie members with suitably compensating turnbuckles.

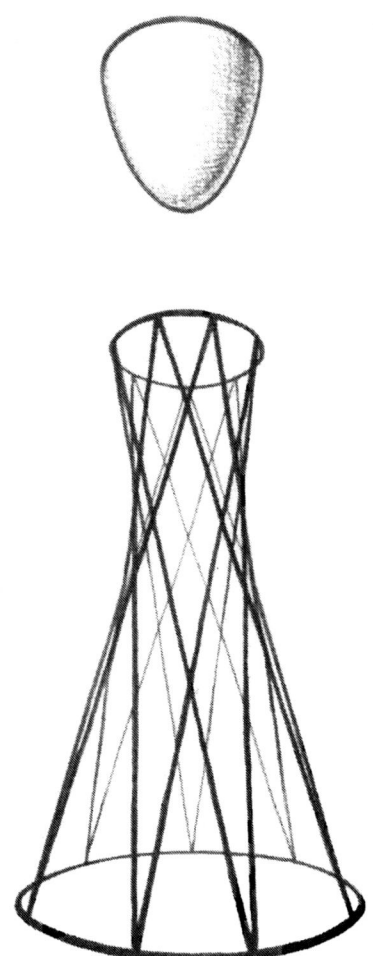

WATER TANKS   Part of the Madrid racecourse project was the construction of two water tanks on the hill overlooking the site. One of these tanks (13,200-gal capacity) was to be at ground level and act as main reservoir. The other, of smaller capacity, was to be elevated and supplied from the lower one so as to provide a suitable pressure head.

Naturally, a structure of some architectural quality was sought, one that would not be out of place with the public stands and with the basic pattern of interplaying hyperboloids in their canopy.

Two hyperboloids are involved in the design shown above. One defines the shape of the elevated tank. The other is the locus of two families of straight lines that correspond to the structure supporting the upper tank. The wall of the lower tank serves as foundation for the entire construction.

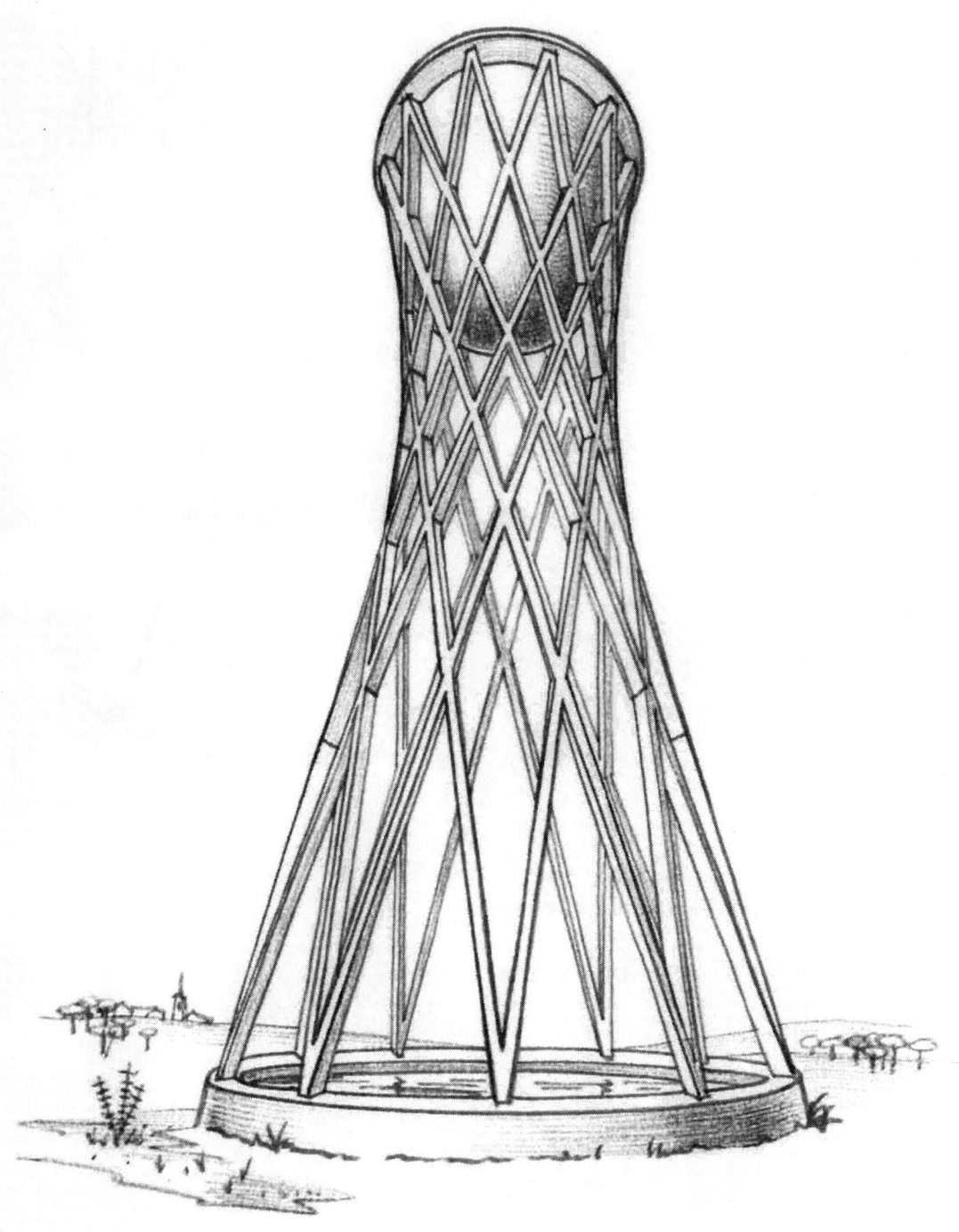

20   *Large Shells*

The tower has a certain appealing quality, and it had been decided to build it. But the war frustrated this dream as it did so many others. The design would have been more expensive to realize than a conventional one, and when the time came to build, circumstances precluded all avoidable expense. The brick structure shown on the following page (cross section below) proved to be cheaper.

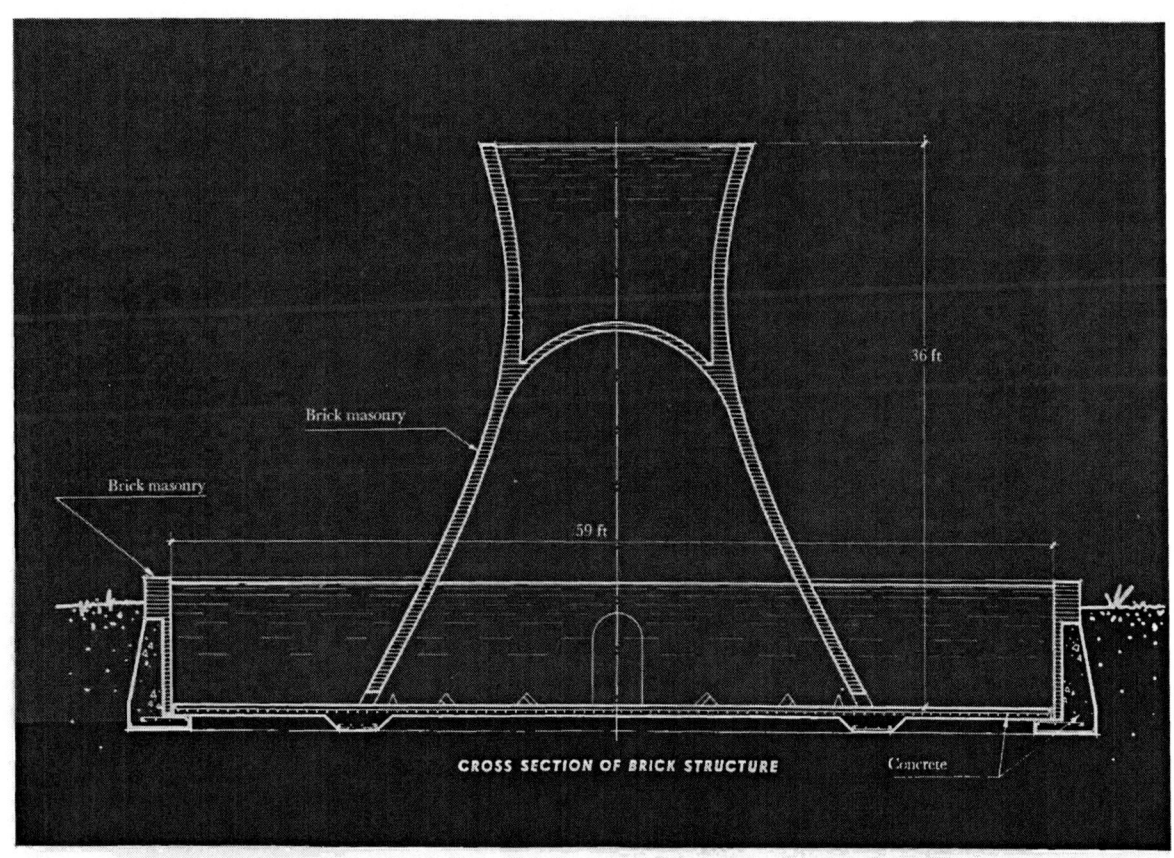

CROSS SECTION OF BRICK STRUCTURE

The passing years have bestowed upon this hyperboloid a certain air of mellow antiquity unforeseen by me; and I still find it beautiful. I realize that this quality and personality reflect time's generous tribute rather than my own merit. Today, looking upon the photograph above, I can hardly recognize the tower as my own and feel inclined to admire it with cold detachment.

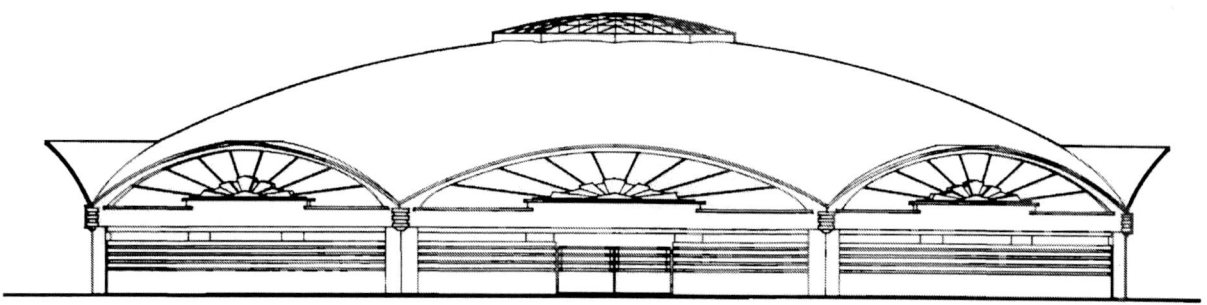

MARKET AT ALGECIRAS
1933

This structure consists of a spherical dome resting on eight peripheral supports. The diameter of the dome is 156 ft, and the radius of curvature is 145 ft.

The outer rim of the dome merges into cylindrical vaults that reach from one support to the next. The joint between the spherical and cylindrical surfaces gives rigidity to the dome and serves to concentrate the principal stresses towards the supports, as can be seen in the diagrams on the following page.

The cylindrical surfaces cantilever beyond the perimeter of supports and thus protect the entrances to the market, which are disposed along the sides of the octagon defined by the eight supports.

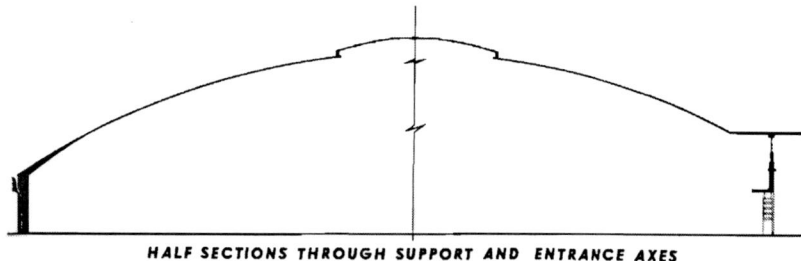

HALF SECTIONS THROUGH SUPPORT AND ENTRANCE AXES

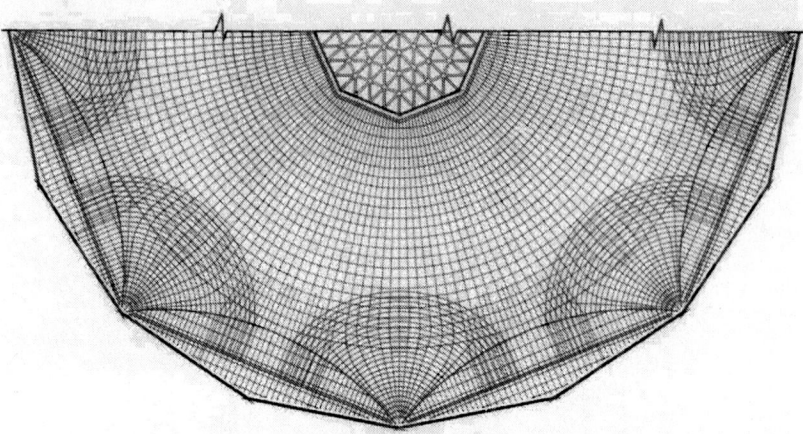

DOME REINFORCEMENT

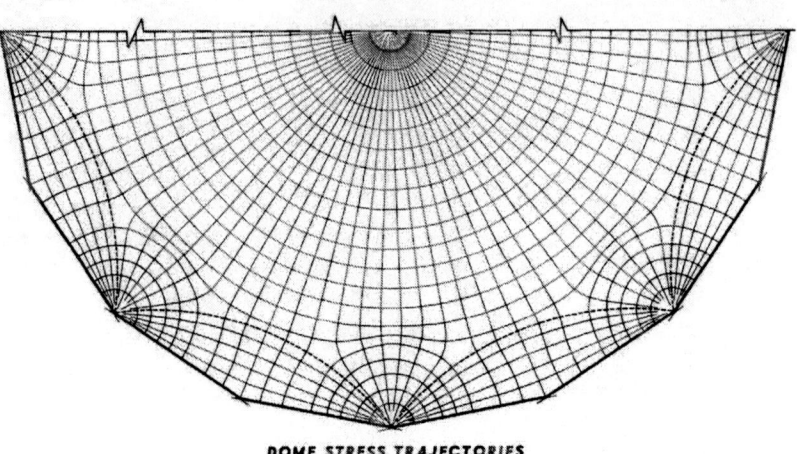

DOME STRESS TRAJECTORIES

The theoretical thickness of the shell is 3.5 in., but the actual thickness increases gradually to 18 in. close to the supports so as to withstand the concentration of forces occurring there. At each of these points the vertical force component is resisted by the support itself, whereas the horizontal radial thrust component is balanced by an octagonal hoop consisting of 16 steel rods, each of 1.2 in. diameter.

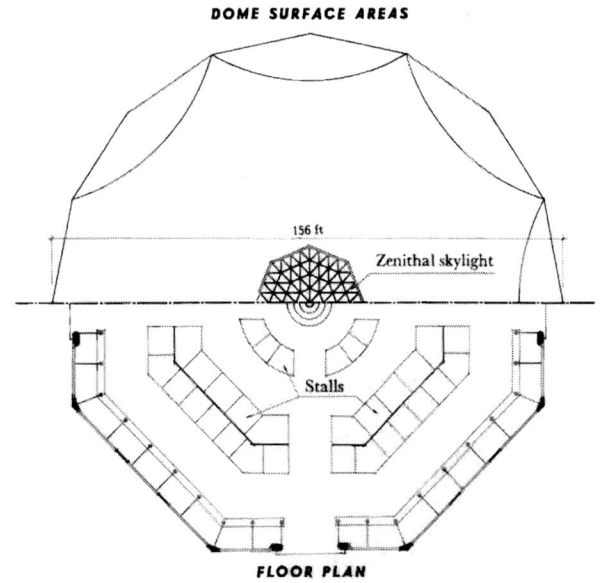

DOME SURFACE AREAS

156 ft

Zenithal skylight

Stalls

FLOOR PLAN

The hoop must stretch to develop stress, whereas the dome, being in compression, tends to contract. Without intervention, this difference could be taken up only by bending of the dome—an inadvisable solution. Hence the hoop rods were provided with turnbuckles so that that they could be shortened and stressed, and the vault in turn compressed in a radial direction at the points of support.

As soon as the hoop had been tightened to the degree estimated necessary, the compressed vault began to lift up and slightly away from the supporting formwork. By thus avoiding the abnormal bending that would have resulted at the removal of the supporting formwork (because of the stretching of the hoop under the outward thrust of the dome), an outward deflection of the top of the supports and the rim of the dome was prevented.

The radial members joining the middle points of each tie member to the vault serve only to stabilize the cylindrical shells and prevent buckling of the edges.

Once its post-tensioning had been completed, the hoop was covered with concrete. This precaution was intended to avoid not only the corrosion of the steel but also any sharp temperature differences between hoop and dome.

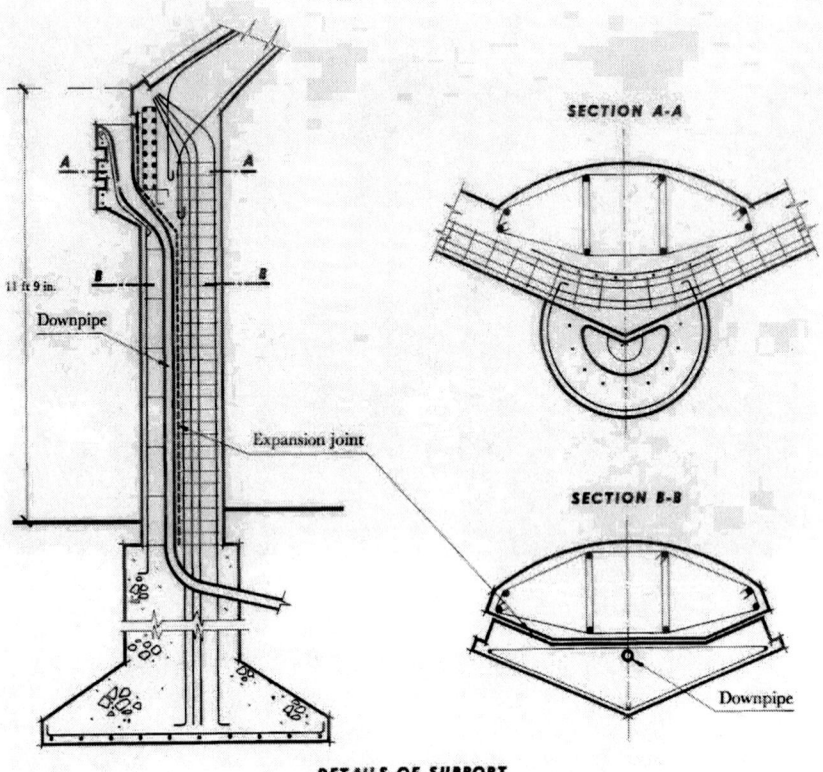

11 ft 9 in.

Downpipe

Expansion joint

Downpipe

DETAILS OF SUPPORT

From this stage onwards, the expansions and contractions of the whole structure do not affect the wall but only the supports, which must allow for radial displacements at the top. So that they may deflect outwards easily and yet withstand tangential shear forces, these supports were designed to be narrow in the radial and wide in the peripheral directions. Thus they insure the stability of the whole structure without being subject to excessive bending moments caused by changes in temperature.

As the entire surface of the roof is in compression, there is no risk of cracking. Thus the dome is watertight and needs no surface or waterproofing treatment.

The market contains a central skylight enclosed within a reinforcement ring. Prefabricated reinforced concrete triangles support the glass panels of the skylight.

The enclosing walls are independent of the structure just described and serve only to enclose the hall.

RAILWAY STATION ROOF
1950

The roof sketched above forms an arch running from the cornice of the station building (already built) to a row of columns running between two railway tracks; it then cantilevers over a second platform.

The whole construction consists of a thin reinforced concrete shell. Because of the longitudinal curvature of each lobe, the roof has sufficient rigidity to function as a beam from the station building to the columns, and beyond these as a cantilever.

The changing curvature of each lobe precludes an exact analysis, but the stresses in the shell can be determined from the study of a reduced scale model. The distribution and dimensions of the reinforcement may then be investigated and the results checked on a reinforced scale model.

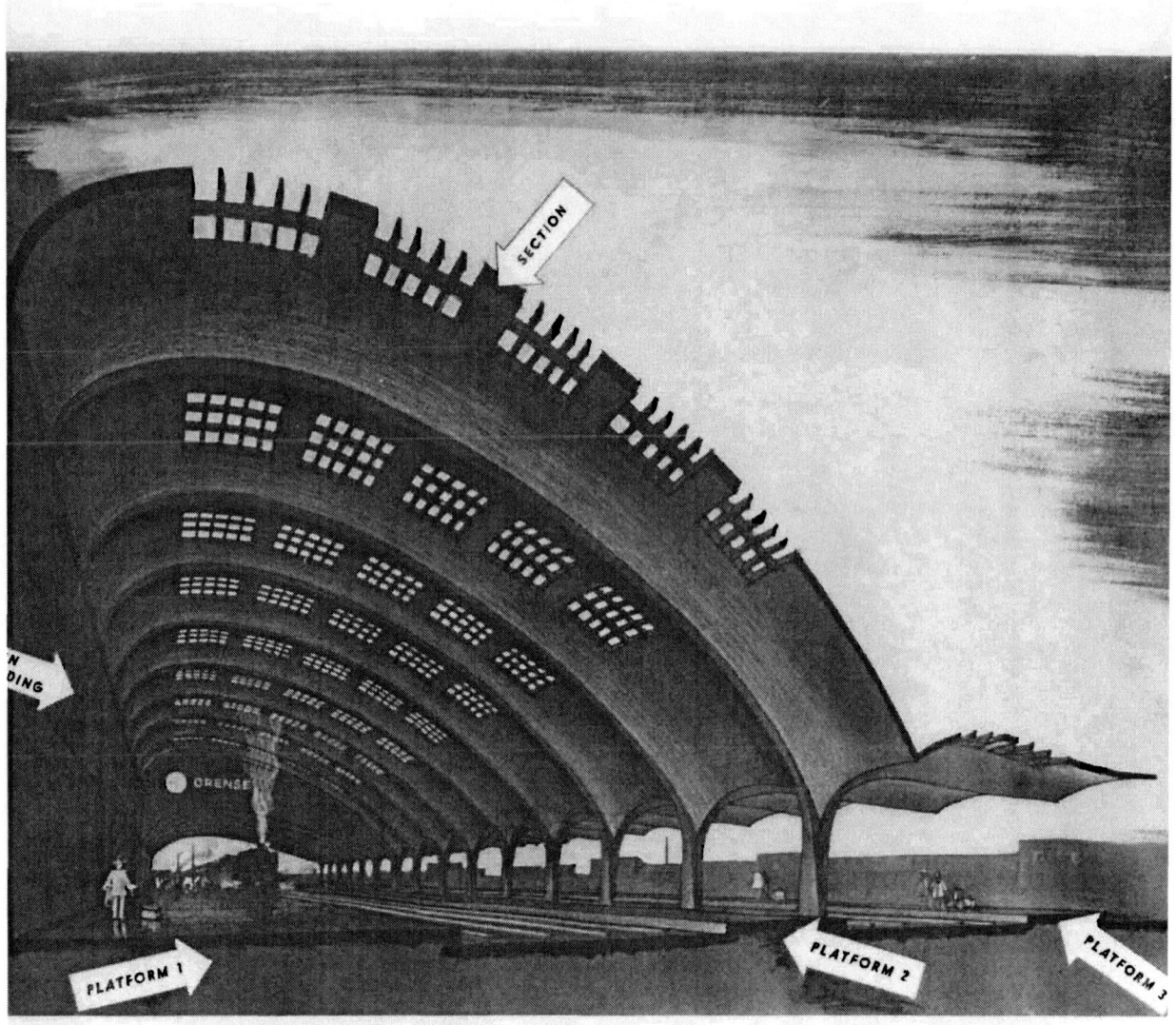

The design, however, was abandoned by the railway company. The continuous roof was supplanted by small marquees cantilevered over each platform from central supports, an arrangement that was obviously cheaper.

Nonetheless, the provisional project may serve to illustrate the great possibilities inherent in this new field of construction, still barely developed—reinforced concrete shells.

FRONTON RECOLETOS
1935

The game of pelota is played on a large rectangular pitch, called a fronton, enclosed by a front, a lateral, and a rear wall (for the rebound of the ball). The spectators mainly occupy the open side facing the lateral wall (see plan below).

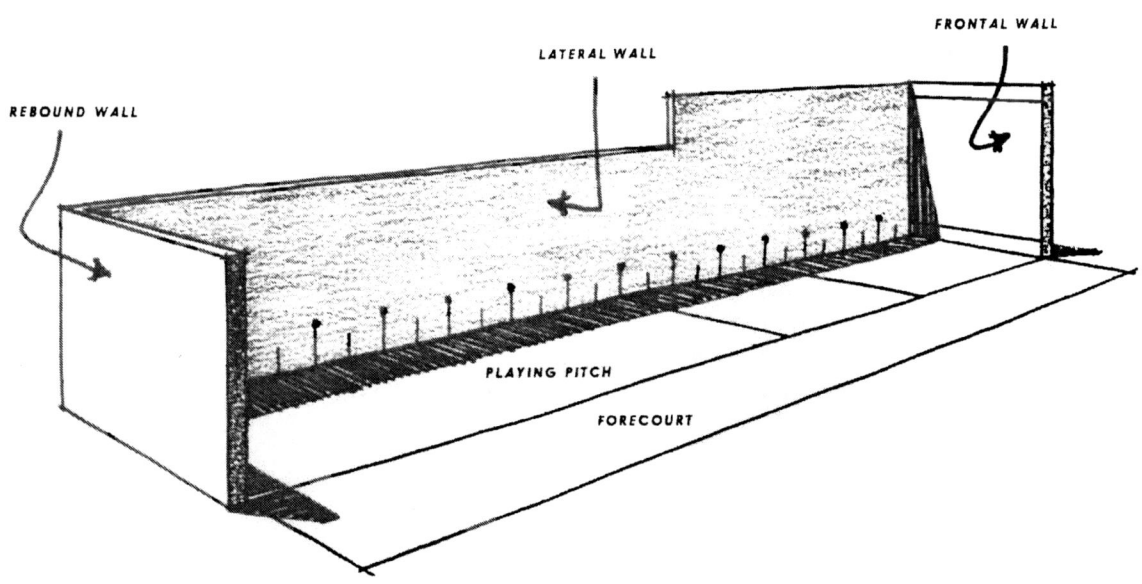

REBOUND WALL

LATERAL WALL

FRONTAL WALL

PLAYING PITCH

FORECOURT

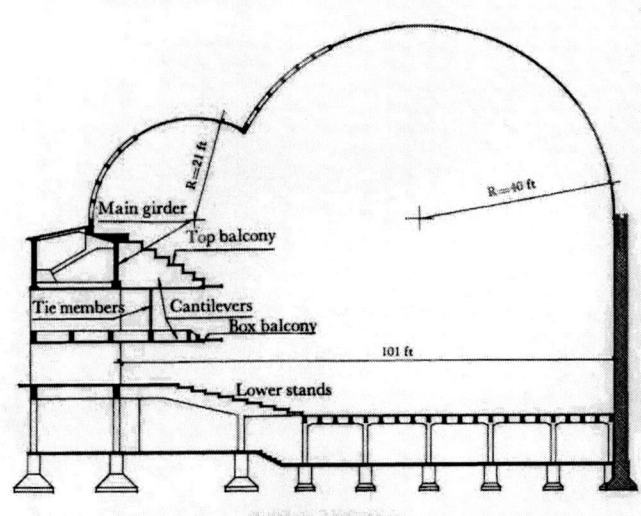

CROSS SECTION

Main girder
$R = 21$ ft
Top balcony
Tie members
Cantilevers
Box balcony
$R = 40$ ft
101 ft
Lower stands

Frontal wall

Lateral wall

53 ft

72 ft   Promenade   Stands   Forecourt   Playing pitch

55 ft

36 ft

Rebound wall

PLAN OF PITCH AND LOWER STANDS

The structure of the lower public stands of the Fronton Recoletos—once the largest fronton in the world of its type—is in itself unremarkable. The top balcony, however, is supported on transverse beams that rest upon and overhang a main longitudinal girder 11½ ft deep and 72 ft long. Hangers from these transverse beams support the lower balcony. This arrangement provides the promenade leading to the ground floor stands with an uninterrupted view of the playing pitch.

Because of the orientation of the hall and the asymmetric arrangement of the playing pitch, it was convenient to design the roof with two skylights facing north. One of them was to provide light for the pitch and the other for the top balcony. Consequently, the exact location in the roof of these skylights was predetermined.

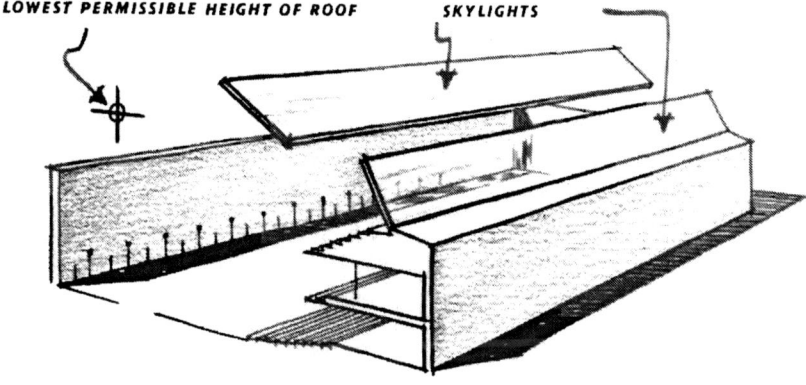

LOWEST PERMISSIBLE HEIGHT OF ROOF   *SKYLIGHTS*

DESIGN DETERMINANTS

Furthermore, the angle of inclination of the skylights was more or less determined by the need to prevent direct sunlight from penetrating into the hall. Their inclination could be increased (as was almost essential for practical reasons) provided their surface could be divided up by horizontal divisions acting as small brise-soleils.

A TRANSVERSE TRUSSED GIRDERS

B LONGITUDINAL GIRDERS

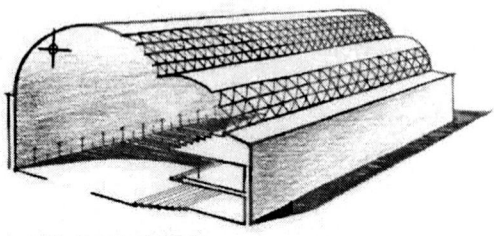

C CYLINDRICAL LOBES

With these limitations, one solution was to arrange a number of transverse trussed girders connected by longitudinal joists (Fig. A). The shape of these trusses, however, proved both structurally and aesthetically unsatisfactory. Another alternative was to place two longitudinal girders across the skylights, thereby making them support the roof (Fig. B). This scheme would have provided the roof with a polygonal cross section, but it also proved to be an unsatisfactory arrangement. The span of the major flat section of the roof would have been too large and required substantial beams for bridging.

Having abandoned these ideas, and remembering the requirements of height and illumination while desiring also to give the greatest possible feeling of spaciousness to the hall, the hand of the imagination instinctively drew out two arcs, the asymmetry of which rhymes with the asymmetry of the hall itself (Fig. C). This profile could be realized by the construction of a cylindrical shell in two lobes. Over the sections occupied by the skylights, the lobes would become a triangulated structure designed for the insertion of glass panes.

Obviously such a shell would be too expensive in normal circumstances because of the large amount of timber necessary for the formwork. The whole shell clearly had to be concreted in one continuous operation, or, at least, the formwork could not be removed until the whole shell had attained a sufficient measure of strength.

However, for this particular project the additional cost was of negligible importance because the completion of the hall was urgently needed for financial reasons. And this very urgency cancelled whatever economic advantages there might have been in adopting another type of structure in which the same formwork could have been used repeatedly for different work areas.

Besides, as the shell was to be very thin, hence very light, the scaffolding did not have to be much more elaborate than that normally needed for workmen to stand on. Furthermore, the contractor had no objection to employing a larger amount of timber, for he could easily reuse it for other contracts he had in hand.

Because of the urgent need to complete the structure, the various levels of the building were concreted without waiting for the formwork of lower levels to be removed; moreover, quick-setting (24-hour) cement was employed for the top balcony and the roof shell. As a result, it was possible to complete work on the whole structure—including excavation, the laying of the foundation, and the removal of formwork—in only 90 working days.

The roof shell consisted of two circular cylindrical sectors joined along a common line parallel to their axes. The radius of the larger cylindrical lobe was 40 ft, that of the smaller, 21 ft. The two surfaces intersected orthogonally.

The total width of the shell roof was 107 ft and the total length, 180 ft. The thickness of the shell was 3⅛ in., except in the neighborhood of the intersection of the two lobes where it increased to 6¼ in. The greater thickness was necessary not only to allow for the larger transverse bending moment in this part of the shell, but also to provide adequate cover for the strong longitudinal reinforcement found there. Incidentally, this reinforcement functioned as the tension chord of a beam with a double curved web. That is to say, the top part of the two lobes corresponded to a compression chord, the intersection of the two lobes to a tension chord, and the part of the lobes close to their intersection to a double web.

Fronton Recoletos   37

REDUCED SCALE MODEL

In the zone of the skylights, the lamina was replaced by a triangulated structure with the same cylindrical shape as the rest of the lobes. These equilateral triangles had sides 4½ ft long; the concrete sections formed by the sides measured 6½ by 12 in.

The shell was calculated by the classical method, which here proved to be considerably more complicated than usual because of the asymmetric form of the lobes and the high position of their intersection in relation to their springing. It involved the assumption of different loading conditions for proper weight, snow, and windage.

Because of the complexity of the design calculations and the ever-present danger of error, the theoretical work was supplemented with an experimental investigation on a reduced scale model (shown above). Later, the strains and deflections of the actual shell were carefully recorded both at the removal of the framework and during the early stages of its life.

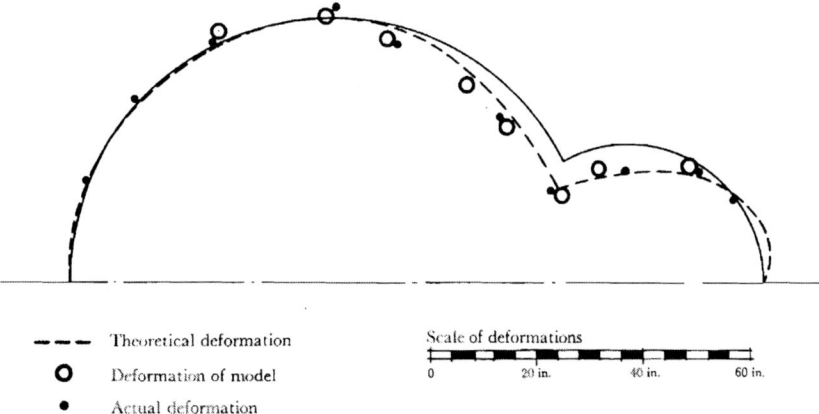

- - - Theoretical deformation

O Deformation of model

● Actual deformation

Scale of deformations

0   20 in.   40 in.   60 in.

COMPARATIVE DEFORMATIONS

The results of these measurements coincided very well with those taken from the model and with the calculated results, except for slight differences due to the greater rigidity and weight of the skylights compared with the rest of the shell (see diagram above). These factors could not be taken into consideration in the theoretical analysis because of the great complications involved.

This fronton was finished a few months before the outbreak of the Spanish Civil War. In the course of this struggle it received a number of direct hits, some of which removed as much as several square yards

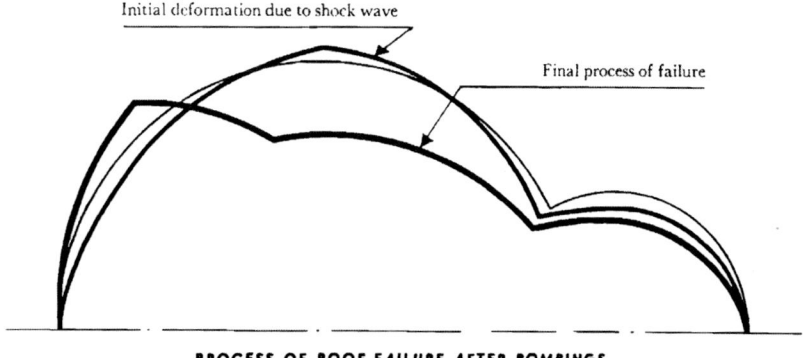

Initial deformation due to shock wave

Final process of failure

PROCESS OF ROOF FAILURE AFTER BOMBINGS

Fronton Recoletos   39

of shell surface. In addition to this damage, aerial bombing must have subjected the structure to severe vibrations. As a consequence, the line of intersection of the two lobes suffered a lateral deflection of over 2 ft and the upper lobe was severely cracked all along the crown. To make matters worse, the longitudinal edges of the top skylight, which were in compression, became curved downwards and developed a pronounced tendency to buckle.

As it was impossible to repair the damage at the time, this buckling grew progressively worse due to the creep or slow deformation of the structure (see page 39). Finally the shell collapsed altogether. Had it been shored without delay and a few reinforcement rings fitted, the building could have been restored to full functional efficiency.

No doubt the collapse of the shell could also have been avoided if these reinforcement rings had been supplied at the time of its erection. Placed on the top side as in the sketch below, they would not have affected its aesthetic aspect nor the total cost. Had I to build it again, I should provide such reinforcement ribs, but unfortunately they would be of little avail against the type of aerial attack that we may expect in the future!

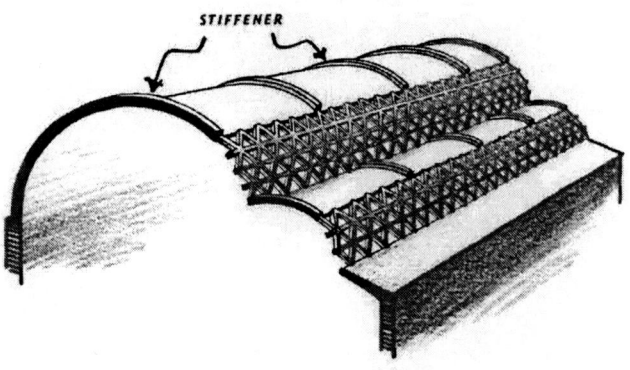

STIFFENER

The top sketch, for a factory in Seville, illustrates the project as it was initially conceived. The traveling cranes would subject the supports to heavy bending loads, which would be increased by windage. It was thought preferable for light to enter through transverse skylights facing north, to prevent direct sunlight. Specifications called for a reinforced concrete structure, as the foundation soil was more than sufficiently solid.

In view of the above circumstances, I considered it preferable to change the initial sketch and make the building independent of the traveling-crane supporting structure (center sketch).

The roof was to consist of lobes, or vaulted shells of double curvature, each independent of the others but integrated into a rigid whole by the frames of the skylights (bottom sketch).

Each lobe was to form a parabolic arch of 280-ft span. Rigidity against possible buckling would be assured by its transverse curvature. The design thickness was to be only 2 in., and the boundary stiffeners were to be 12 x 18 in.

INITIAL DESIGN

FINAL DESIGN

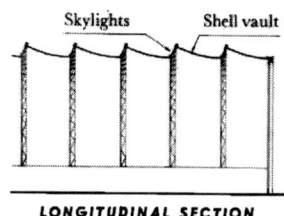

LONGITUDINAL SECTION

41

The top boundary of one lobe was to be joined to the lower boundary of the next by metal bars forming a triangular pattern. These would give rigidity and strength in bending to the arch under the compression and suction forces of the wind. The metal triangles would also serve to support the glass panes.

The trumpetlike shape of each shell vault would make it possible to shift the formwork along rails to the position of the next lobe. Once the formwork for this new lobe had been placed, the bars of the skylight would be fitted and the lobe concreted.

The estimated cost for this design was 20 per cent less than that for the original and more conventional project, but the plan was turned down, perhaps because it semed too revolutionary.

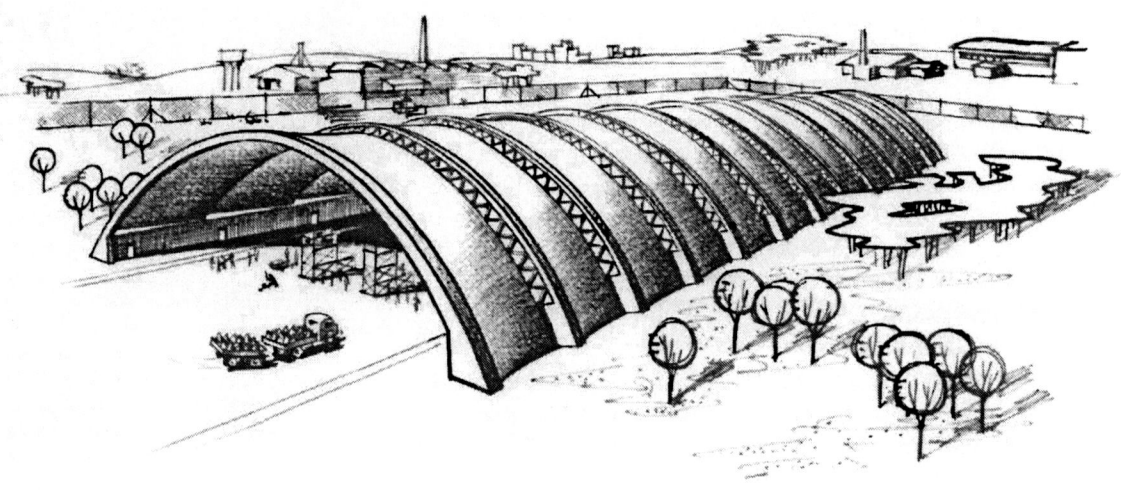

SPECIAL SHELL ROOF FOR THE TACHIRA CLUB
1957

Although the outline shown in the first sketch was initially chosen by the architect, that of the second was finally considered preferable.

To simplify construction, the directrixes are parallel and identical in shape. Their apexes run along a line of double curvature in space.

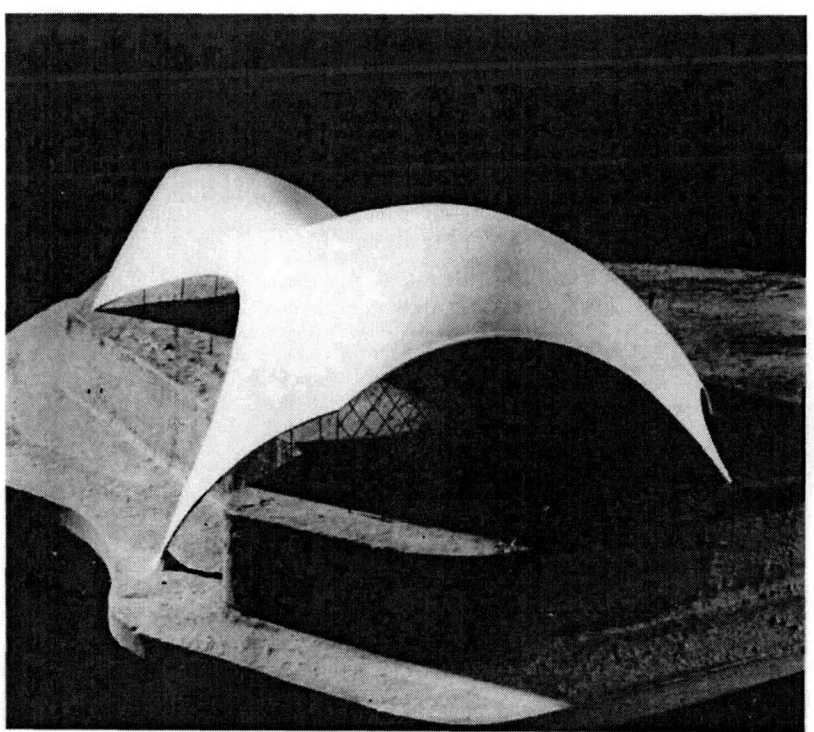

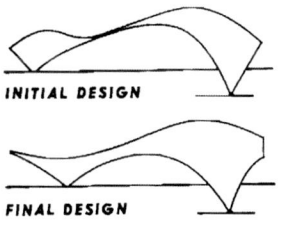

INITIAL DESIGN

FINAL DESIGN

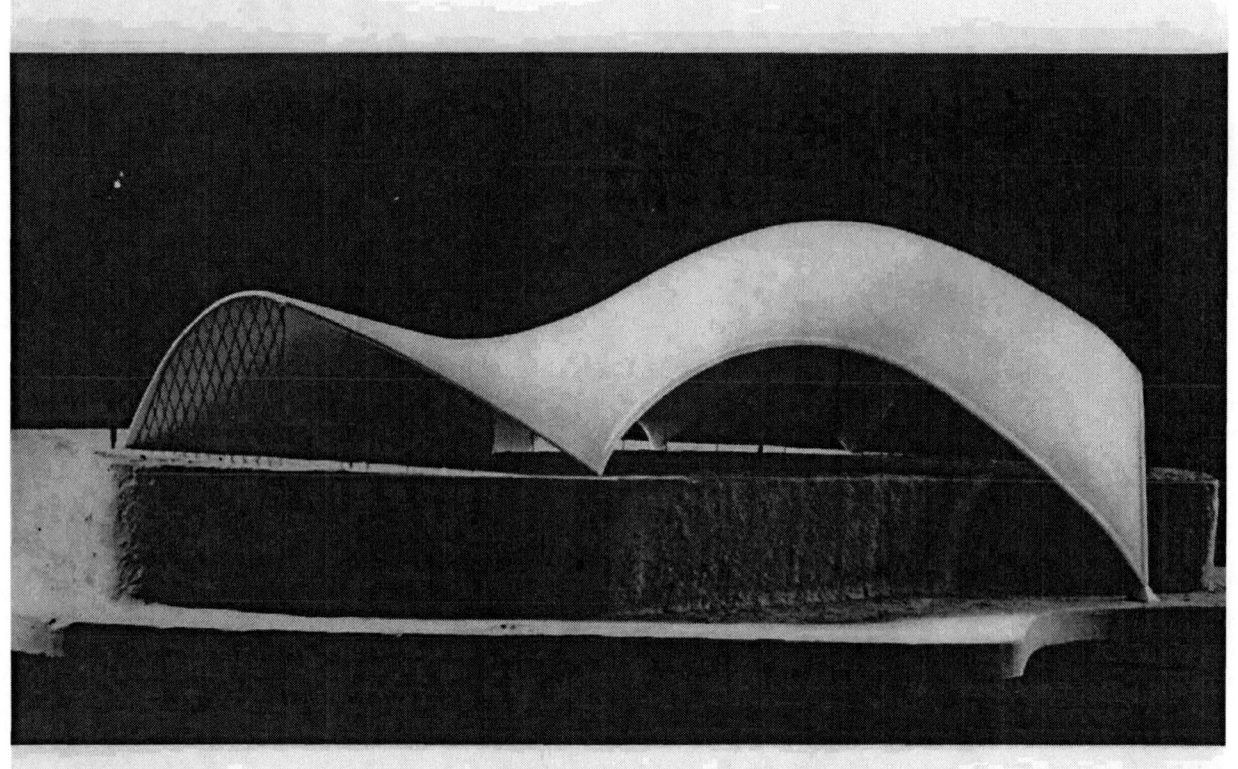

The shell so determined is cut by arches made rigid by vertical and very thin ties that provide the most unobstructed possible view of the valley. The climate of the region (Caracas, Venezuela) is such that this facade can be left wide open.

The thrust of the vault is transmitted by the shell itself—which is slightly reinforced along its boundary—to the extremities of the half arch. No compression loads are induced on the vertical members. The side boundaries are stabilized by reticular glass-paneled facades.

The shell is designed for a constant thickness of 4 in. and will support an external mosaic facing and an inner soundproofing material.

To avoid harmful shrinkage effects, the continuous foundation of

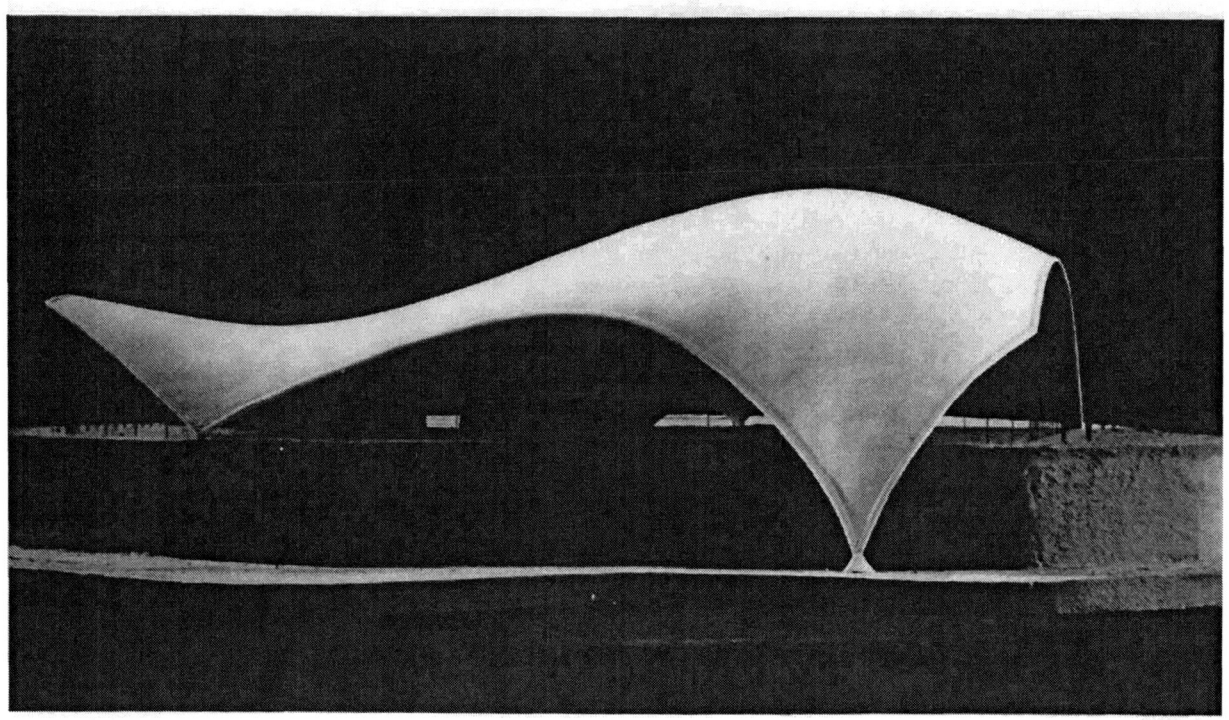

the rear side rests on roller bearings and connecting rods. The latter resist the horizontal thrusts at floor level.

Longitudinal prestressing above the roller bearings prevents cracking. The two support points of the main arch are linked by horizontal tie members to a central anchorage mass (see following page). This mass is also attached to the flooring slab, which contains horizontal reinforcements that run to the connecting rods over the roller bearings in order to resist their horizontal thrust. Thereby all horizontal thrusts are counterbalanced, and the ground, whose properties had been found unreliable for resisting horizontal forces, supports merely vertical loads.

To supplement the approximate calculations by which the shape of the shell and its main dimensions were fixed, a model to the scale of 1:10 was tested at the Central Structural Materials Testing Laboratory in Madrid. The model was made of reinforced mortar and loaded by means of a large number of floaters suspended from the shell. The weight of the floaters could be uniformly varied by changing the water level of the tank in which they floated. The shell roof was also tested for an uneven load on one side with respect to the other, as a simulation of windage. Still another test reproduced the effect on the stress distribution of a temperature difference between the inner and outer faces of the shell roof when artificially heated. Maximum stresses in the actual shell are not more than 112 psi.

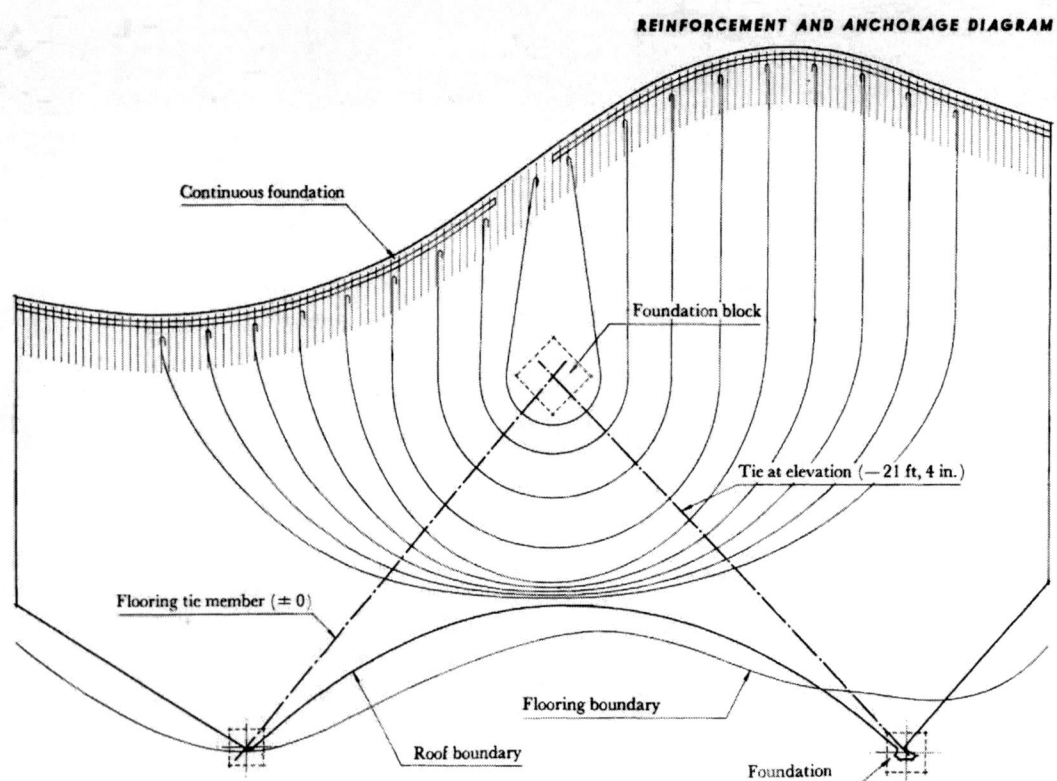

REINFORCEMENT AND ANCHORAGE DIAGRAM

Continuous foundation

Foundation block

Tie at elevation (— 21 ft, 4 in.)

Flooring tie member (± 0)

Flooring boundary

Roof boundary

Foundation

2 VIADUCTS AND AQUEDUCTS

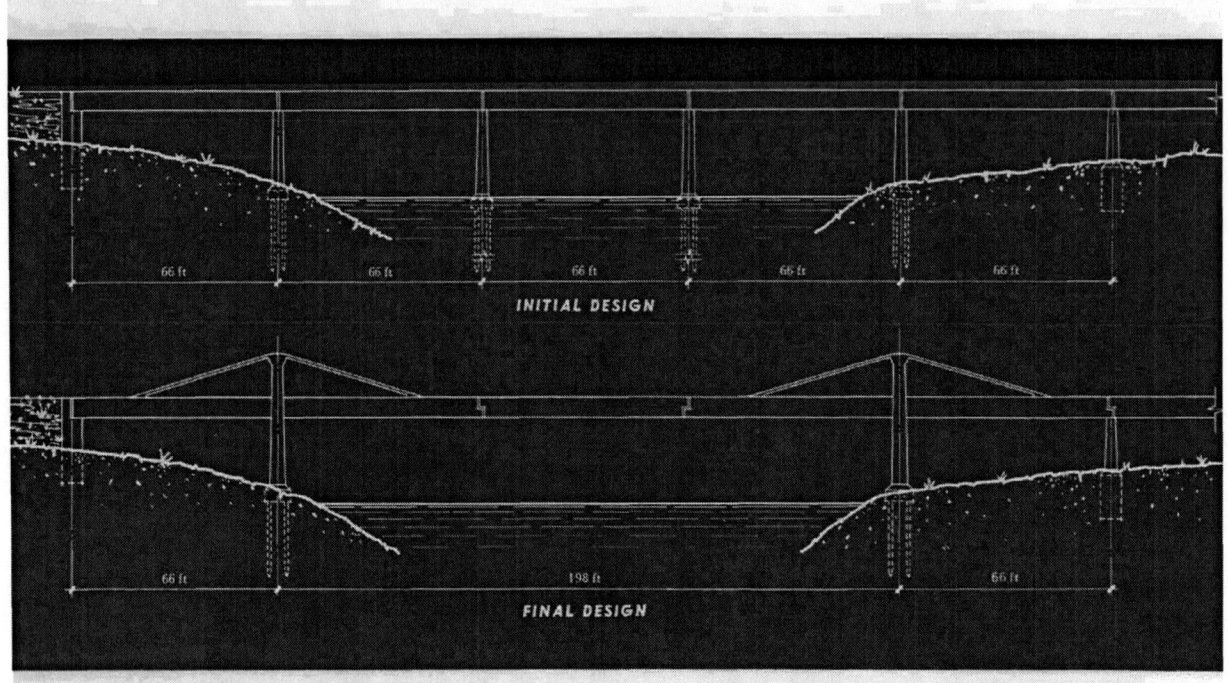

INITIAL DESIGN

FINAL DESIGN

66 ft 66 ft 66 ft 66 ft 66 ft 66 ft

66 ft 198 ft 66 ft

TEMPUL AQUEDUCT
1925

The inhabitants of Jerez de la Frontera, that ancient city famous for the noble Spanish sherries, must sometimes also drink water. And the provision of water for the city involved the construction of an aqueduct over the Guadalete river bed.

The first project consisted of fourteen 66-ft spans to be supported on piers with foundations reaching 13 ft into the ground. This type of construction was to extend over the section of the river bed that is under water only during flood periods, whereas the three spans bridging the actual water course were to be supported by foundations consisting of piles 33 ft deep. This arrangement was selected in order to avoid the expensive drainage necessary when foundations are constructed by means of underwater wells. The spans were to consist of rectangular box sections accommodating the water conduits inside.

When the project was submitted for approval, the contracting authorities insisted that the foundations of the two piers in the deepest part of the water might be undermined. I was pressed for time and wanted to find without delay an alternative design that would interfere as little as possible with the existing project. I therefore decided to maintain the same spans except for the two river piers. These were to be replaced by two tie members that would run across the bankside piers—after these had been suitably increased in height—and be anchored close to the next two piers. Thus it would suffice to strengthen the foundations of the bankside piers, reinforcing them with the piles saved up from the two eliminated river piers.

The design had the advantage of being able to be constructed in a few summer months. It was soon accepted by the authorities, and work started immediately afterwards.

The tie members, including the anchorage, were to be about 135 ft

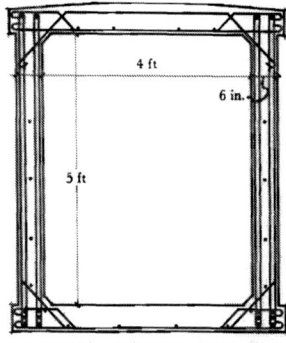

TYPICAL CROSS SECTION

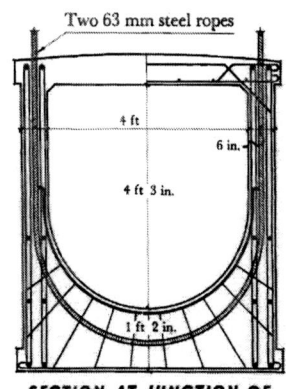

SECTION AT JUNCTION OF STEEL ROPES AND SPAN

49

VIEW OF AQUEDUCT DURING FLOOD

long. In 1926, however, there was no prestressing technique available to handle such lengths, nor was welding sufficiently advanced to trust to it a structure of this importance. The classical method of joining bars by overlapping them within concrete was not satisfactory either. Consequently, I decided to use twisted cables of high tensile steel. With these, tie members could be easily made in one piece and conveniently transported in the conventional manner, rolled up in drums. They would also have the advantage of being simple to unwind and place in position at the working site.

The only difficulty to be overcome was the considerable elongation of the cables at loading. The solution consisted in supporting the cables at the top of the piers on independent seatings as shown on the opposite page. Thus, once the overhanging spans anchoring the ends of the cables had been concreted, the height of these seatings could be lifted by means of hydraulic jacks. The additional elevation would stretch the cables until they reached their proper working stress.

In fact, it so happened that just as the concreting of the spans was nearly finished and the concrete had reached an adequate strength, a heavy flood began to wash away the timber centering (view above shows aqueduct under similar flood conditions). In this emergency it sufficed to operate the jacks, thereby lifting the seating of the cables 10 in. As a result, the cables became sufficiently taut to lift the overhanging spans slightly (about 2 in. at the tips) and thus separate the concrete structure from the centering, which was left to the mercy of the surging waters.

A few weeks later when the spans had been fully overloaded, the space between the top of the piers and seating of the cables was concreted and the jacks removed. The empty space left by the jacks was also filled with concrete, and finally the cables themselves were encased in concrete to avoid the risk of corrosion.

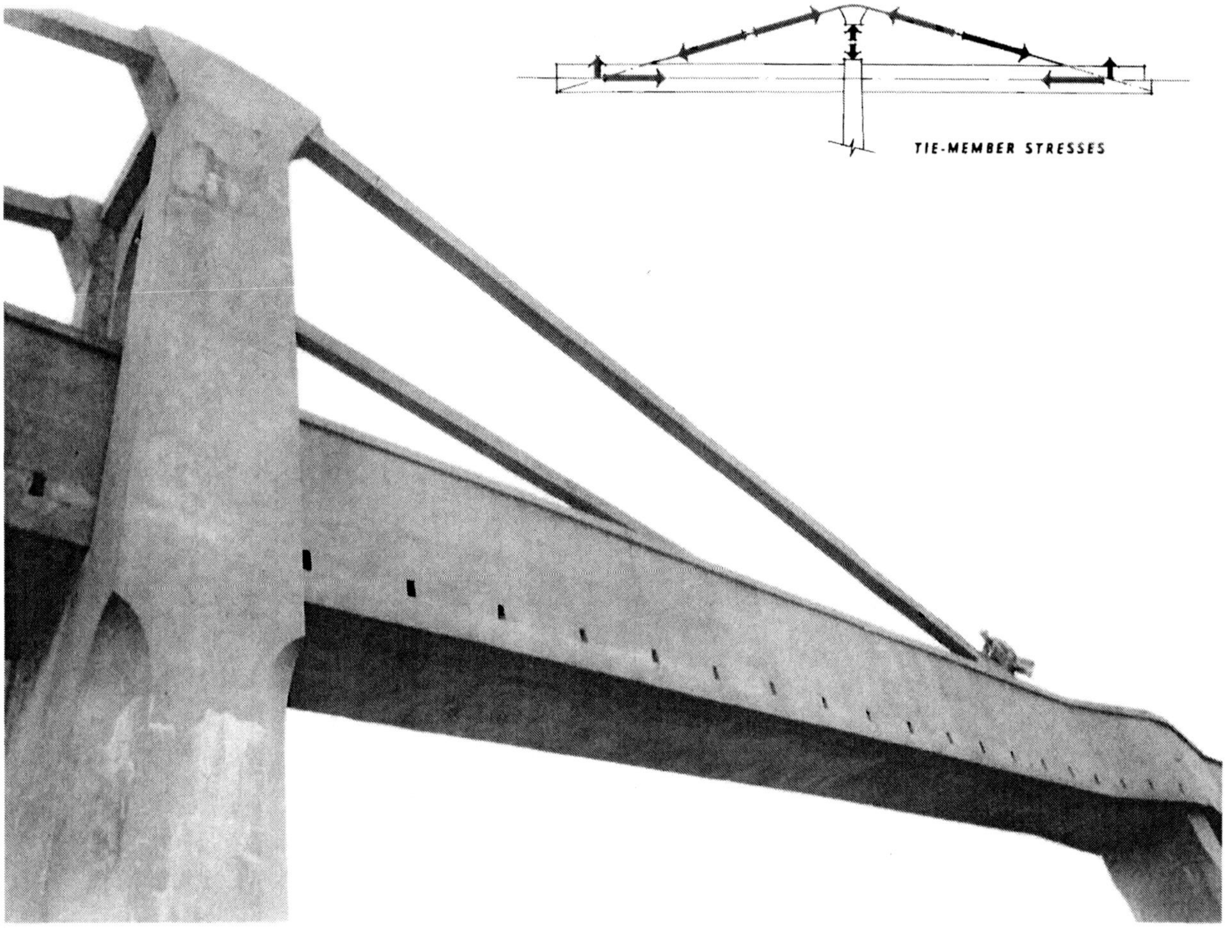

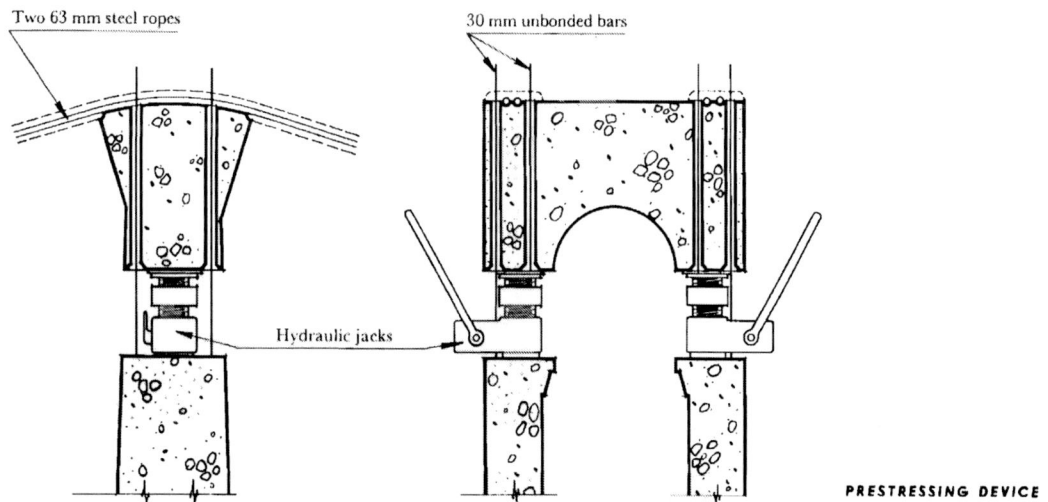

TIE-MEMBER STRESSES

Two 63 mm steel ropes

30 mm unbonded bars

Hydraulic jacks

PRESTRESSING DEVICE

Tempul Aqueduct   51

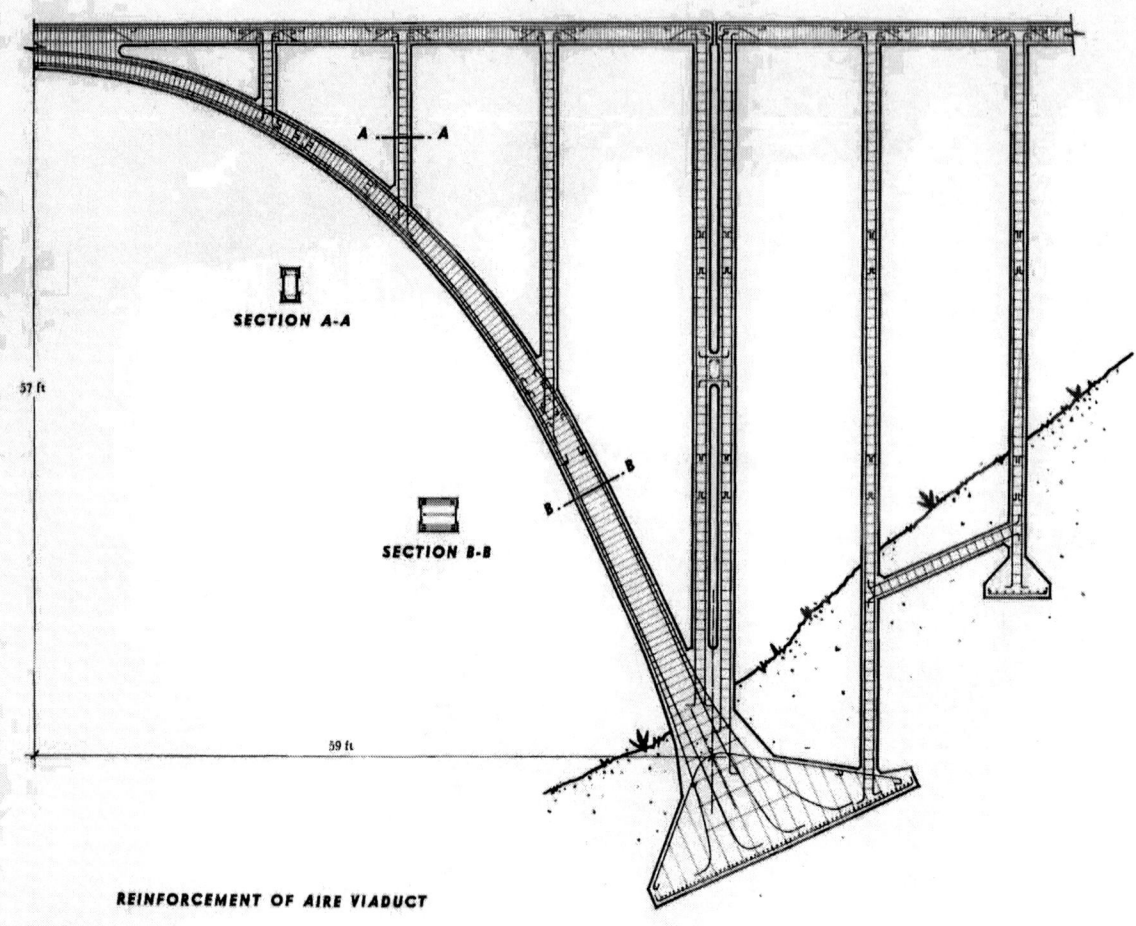

57 ft

59 ft

A .... A

SECTION A-A

B .... B

SECTION B-B

REINFORCEMENT OF AIRE VIADUCT

52

VIADUCTS AT MADRID UNIVERSITY CITY
1933

AIRE VIADUCT   The Aire Viaduct with its twin arches of 118-ft span does not exhibit any special structural features, but it does have a certain latticelike grace. The slenderness of the spandrel columns permits them to take up the transverse deflections caused by the expansion of the deck.

The spans between these columns are not all equal. Those between the shorter columns are slightly smaller to improve the optical effect of the proportions.

The stress calculation of the arch was made by a graphical application of the ellipse of inertia method.

53

54   *Viaducts and Aqueducts*

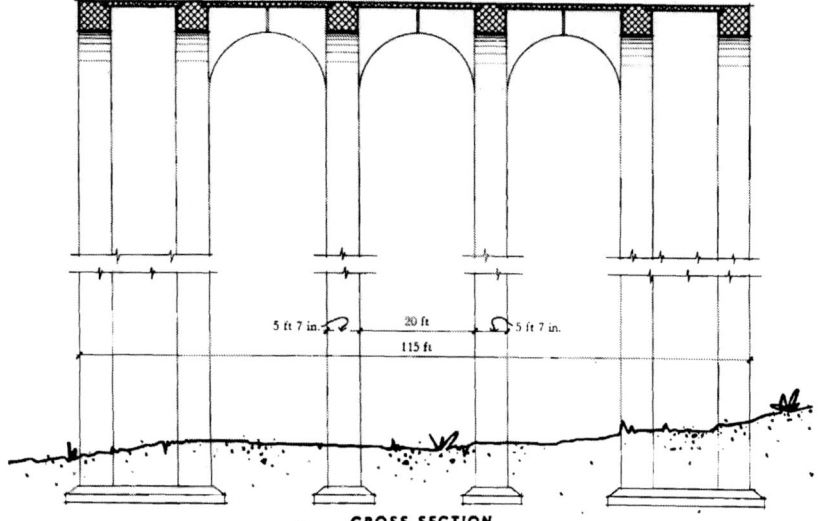

CROSS SECTION

5 ft 7 in.   20 ft   5 ft 7 in.

115 ft

QUINCE OJOS VIADUCT   The Quince Ojos Viaduct consists of a multiple arcade of 25 arches, each 25 ft 7 in. in span. The piers are 5 ft 7 in. wide. The transverse arches are similar to the longitudinal ones. The total width of the viaduct is 115 ft.

The great length and rigidity of this structure made it essential to place expansion joints at frequent intervals and in places where they would not spoil its appearance. It was therefore decided—as the least undesirable solution—to situate the joints exactly at the arch crowns (see cross section). This positioning transformed the arches into double cantilevers.

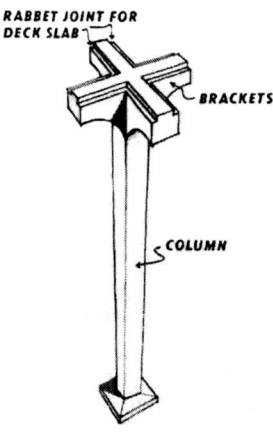

RABBET JOINT FOR
DECK SLAB

BRACKETS

COLUMN

56   *Viaducts and Aqueducts*

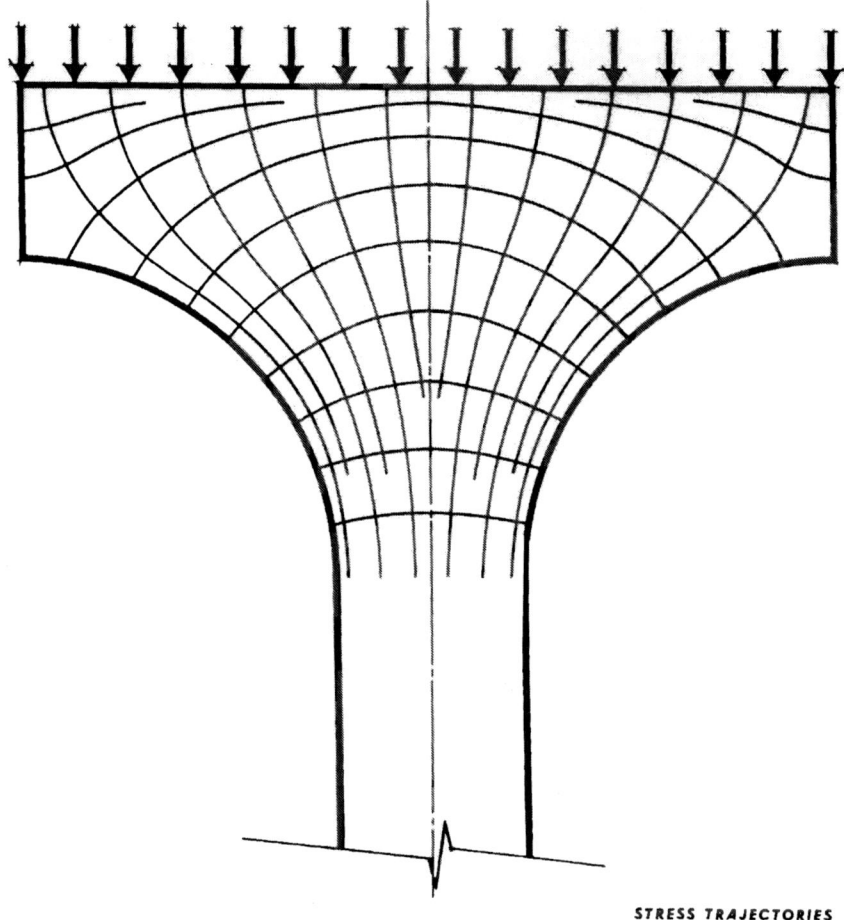

STRESS TRAJECTORIES

The viaduct thus consists of a series of structural units, each one a slender pier at the top of which four symmetrical cantilevered half arches branch out. These half arches, in conjunction with those of adjoining piers, form square frames and support the square slabs that make up the deck.

The superficial impression that the viaduct is a series of arches instead of separate cantilevers might be interpreted as a weakness. But in fact, what is the actual structural function of these cantilevers? A photoelastic analysis shows the stress distribution to be as in the sketch above, and this distribution is certainly no less functional than it would be in an arch.

ALLOZ AQUEDUCT
1939

The fundamental idea in the design of this aqueduct was the elimination of any possibility of fissuration or water infiltration through the channel walls by subjecting them to two-way compression on their inside face.

To achieve the desired result, the aqueduct was made up of sections 124 ft long and supported on legs spaced every 62 ft, with each section cantilevered 31 ft at both ends. The bending moments due to the weight of the water channel are therefore negative throughout the whole length of each section except at the free ends and at the midpoint, where they are zero. They are highest over the supports (see diagram, following page). As these negative bending moments induce tensile stresses in the top part of the section, the channel was posttensioned. The resultant stress is a longitudinal compression that extends over the whole channel section and is greatest towards the bottom, where the liquid pressure is also greatest (see diagram, following page).

To compress the inside face of the channel transversely, a number of

59

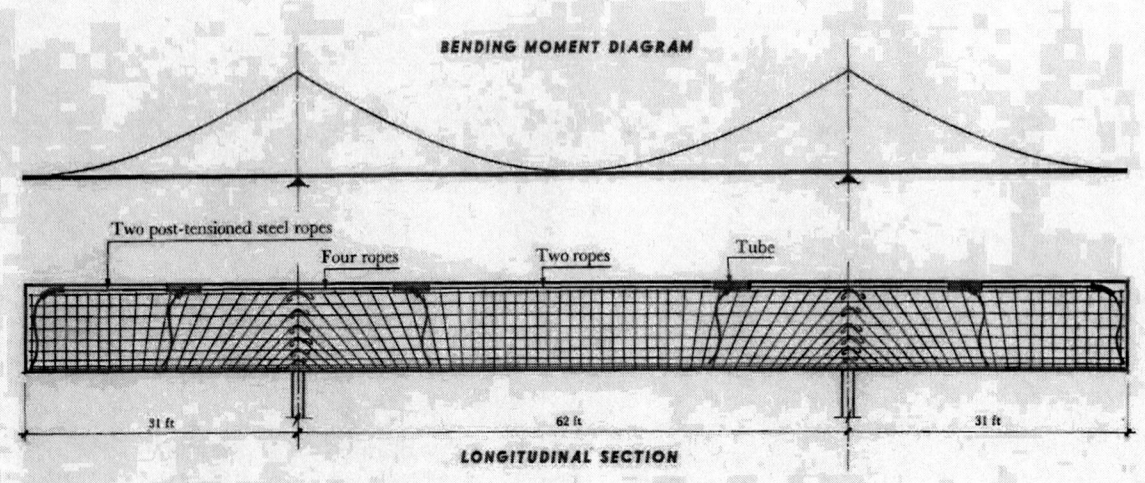

BENDING MOMENT DIAGRAM

Two post-tensioned steel ropes

Four ropes   Two ropes   Tube

31 ft   62 ft   31 ft

LONGITUDINAL SECTION

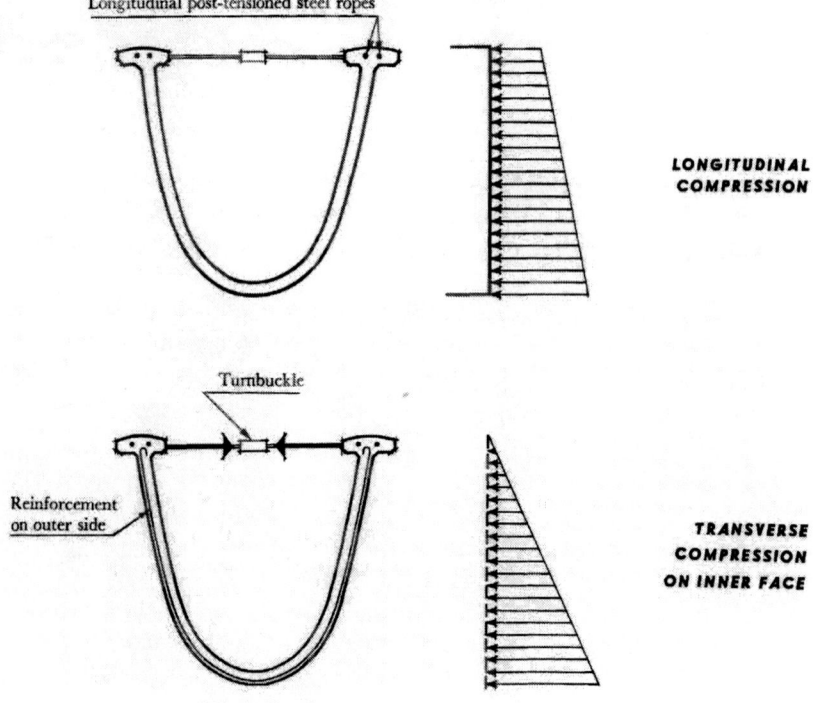

Longitudinal post-tensioned steel ropes

LONGITUDINAL
COMPRESSION

Turnbuckle

Reinforcement
on outer side

TRANSVERSE
COMPRESSION
ON INNER FACE

60   *Viaducts and Aqueducts*

cross bars were fitted to connect the opposite top edges of the U-shaped channel. These bars were placed at 15-ft intervals and tightened by means of turnbuckles. The tightening tended to pull the lateral walls closer together, and the resultant transverse bending moments put them in compression in the inner face, the compressive stress increasing towards the bottom.

The transverse reinforcement running close to the outer side of the channel walls works in tension under these bending moments. This reinforcement also transmits the shear forces from the overhanging part of the channel along its sides to the legs, and supports the bottom of the channel under the stress of its sides, which function as the full webs of a U-shaped beam.

To facilitate the longitudinal post-tensioning, two pair of steel ropes —supplemented by an additional two over each support section—were placed along the shallow channels that form the free edges of the U channel. These shallow channels also serve as service catwalks and as rigid beams (resisting bending in a horizontal plane) between the cross bars.

These longitudinal steel ropes were anchored at the extremities of each channel section as soon as it was concreted. As the cables were made up of twisted wire, good anchorage was achieved simply by separating the wires and twisting their ends into hooks. The tubes shown in the diagrams prevent undesirable bonding between the cables and the concrete close to the latter's surface.

ANCHORAGE OF LONGITUDINAL CABLES

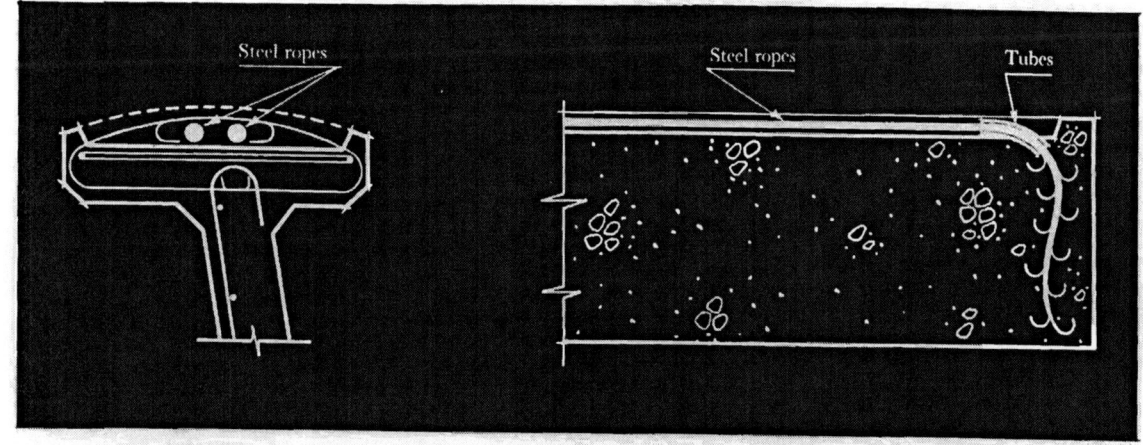

Once the concrete had hardened adequately, each pair of cables was stretched in the following manner. The two steel ropes were clamped together at two neighboring points. Then, midway between the two clamps, the cables were forced apart, thus bringing the clamped positions closer together and stretching the cables longitudinally. This operation was easily performed with the help of a pair of pivoted levers operated by a small hydraulic jack. When the required tension in the cables had been reached, they were kept permanently apart by a spreader (see diagram at top of opposite page).

Whenever the maximum possible separation of the two cables allowed by the size of the box did not prove sufficient (measured by the load on the hydraulic jack), the same procedure was repeated on a different section of the same pair of cables.

After the cables had been post-tensioned in the manner just described, they were covered with sand for protection against the atmosphere and particularly from solar radiation. After a few weeks the jacked levers were again applied to check their load. The load was readjusted wherever slackening had occurred because of the creep of the steel or the shrinkage of the concrete.

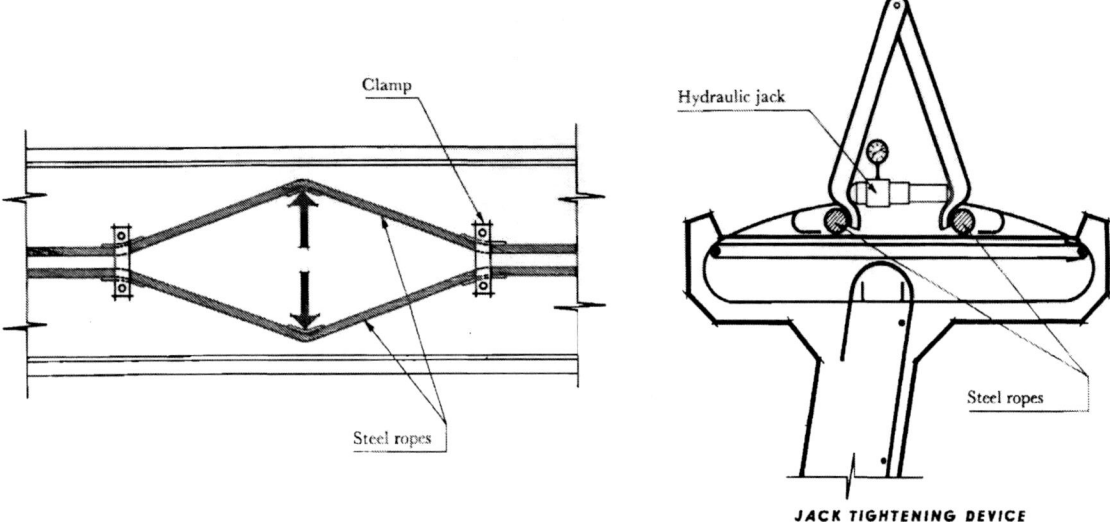

Clamp

Steel ropes

Hydraulic jack

Steel ropes

JACK TIGHTENING DEVICE

After this second stretching adjustment, the cables were encased in concrete, and the joints between each section of the viaduct were sealed by means of lead sheets fixed into the concrete and covered with bituminous mastic stiffened by wire mesh (cross section below).

The supports of the viaduct consist of two inclined legs, resembling gigantic compasses, that give the assembly a certain stylishness and insure full stability.

These supports extend around the channel and help to reinforce it at the point where it is supported. As the U section of the channel became slightly closed on the tightening of the cross bars, the top part of the supports (also U-shaped) was provided with special cuts or joints so that it could deflect with the channel section.

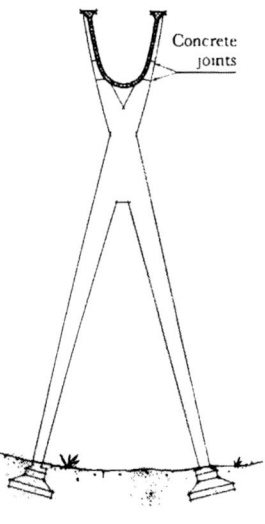

Concrete joints

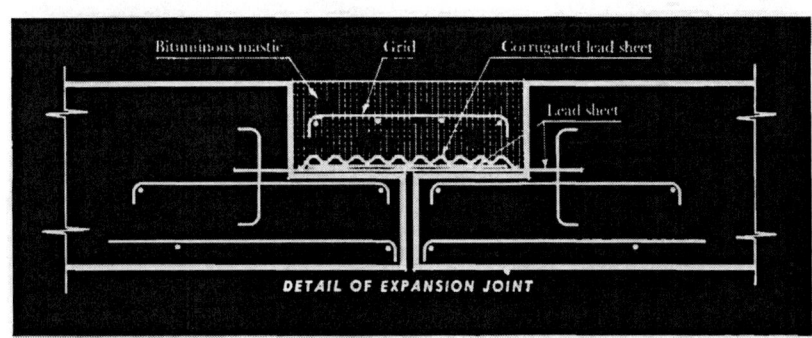

Bituminous mastic   Grid   Corrugated lead sheet

Lead sheet

DETAIL OF EXPANSION JOINT

64   *Viaducts and Aqueducts*

CHANNEL SECTION SHOWING TRANSVERSE REINFORCEMENT

The structural behavior of the channel both in its cantilevered and central span sections is that of cylindrical shells. The half cross section of the channel was given the shape of a third-degree parabola; this provides a good hydraulic contour and has satisfactory structural properties.

The total length of the various aqueduct sections comes to 1,340 ft. In none of them has there been any sign of cracks or leakage, despite the fact all construction details were accomplished easily and cheaply.

PROJECT FOR A HALF-MILE AQUEDUCT
1956

The problem here was similar to that of the aqueduct of Alloz, previously described, except for the greater length involved—approximately 3,000 ft. This counselled a reduction in the cost of the longitudinal post-tensioning that would be necessary for eliminating tensile stresses caused by bending of the spans. Furthermore, the condition had been made that there be as few expansion joints as possible. This restriction suggested a continuous beam across a large number of equal spans, thereby obtaining the additional advantage of considerably reduced bending moments.

Consequently, it was finally decided to fit a single joint in the center of the aqueduct to connect two continuous beams fixed-ended at the two extremities of the viaduct. Over this central joint, a three-hinged arch was mounted on the aqueduct beam. This arch applies on each side of the joint a constant horizontal thrust of 400 tons, which has the effect of a compression force all along the aqueduct. The arrangement is cheaper than the system of prestressed cables customarily used for the same purpose. The saving in cost is greater in proportion to the length of the structural elements to be compressed.

To insure constant longitudinal thrust whatever the size of the aperture at the joint, the two surfaces of contact at the central hinge are provided with the necessary curvature. Thus the point of contact will always be at the same given height whether the arch springers move closer together or further apart under the effects of temperature changes and the elastic and plastic deformations along the full length of the aqueduct.

67

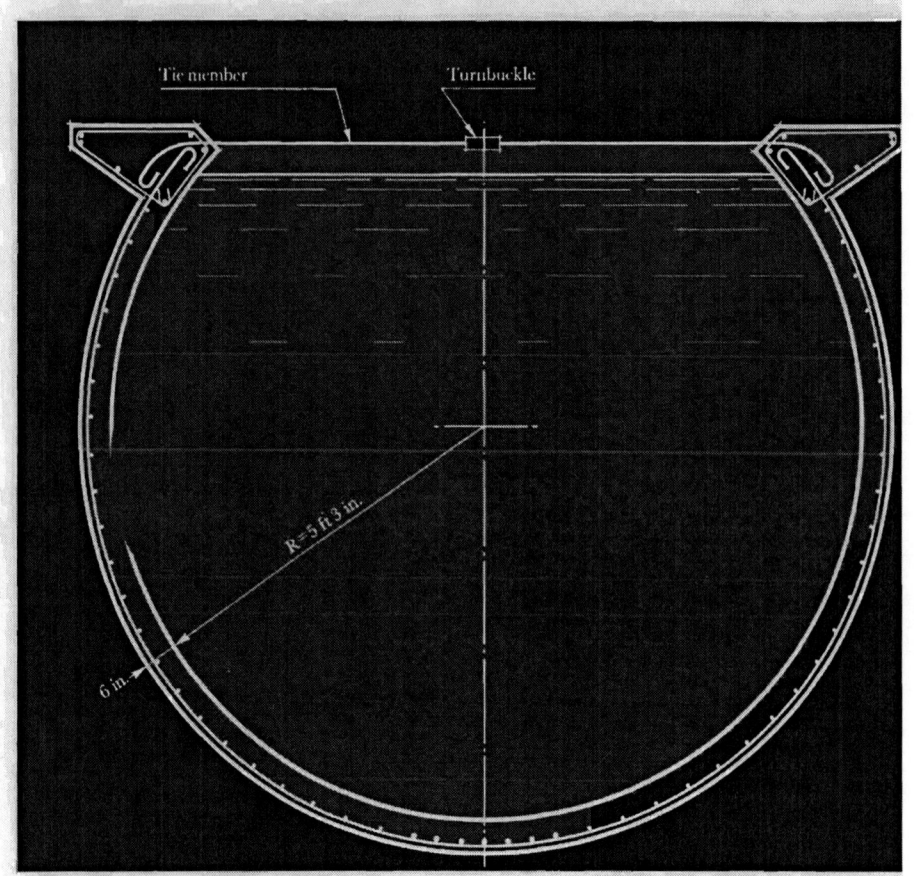

The piles were designed with the necessary transverse rigidity to prevent buckling in the beam but at the same time they are two-hinged to provide free beam expansion and shrinkage without noticeably impeding the longitudinal transmission of the compression induced by the arch.

The waterproofing of the joint is provided for on the inner surface of the channel by rubber sheets and on the outer surface by a metal sleeve which goes across the joint, thus allowing for its free expansion.

Half-Mile Aqueduct   69

The main approaches to the viaduct and the timber cocket centering over which this great arch was to be concreted had already been erected when the Spanish Civil War disrupted the progress of the work.

The harshness of the climate on the Castilian-Leonese plateau, however, made further use of this centering practically impossible, for it had been subjected for three years to cold, humid gales in winter and a baking sun in summer.

The arch to be constructed had a 690-ft span. The crown was to be 165 ft above the reservoir water level and 330 ft above the ground. It was necessary, therefore, to search for a type of full-span arched centering that could support the weight of the concrete of the final arch at a reasonable cost.

Moreover, one of the conditions of the job was that the appearance and the main plans prepared for the initial project by the deceased engineer Martin Gil (whose name has been given to the viaduct) should not be modified. At the time, in fact, the arch was of world-record size in concrete. Even now, it is surpassed in size only by the Sando arch in Sweden. The chief problem, therefore, was to determine the most satisfactory method of constructing such a vast structure.

It has now become standard practice to place the centering inside the arch to be constructed. The centering is also so designed that after its initial purpose has been served, it can continue to function effectively as permanent reinforcement of the concrete. For this second purpose, less steel is generally needed than is for the actual centering of the arch. Consequently it is important to study the method of concreting carefully so that the lightest possible centering will suffice.

To this end, the Esla Arch was concreted in longitudinal strips, or

71

layers. The final layers were made heavier than the initial ones because the strength of these had increased the ability of the centering to support the additional weight.

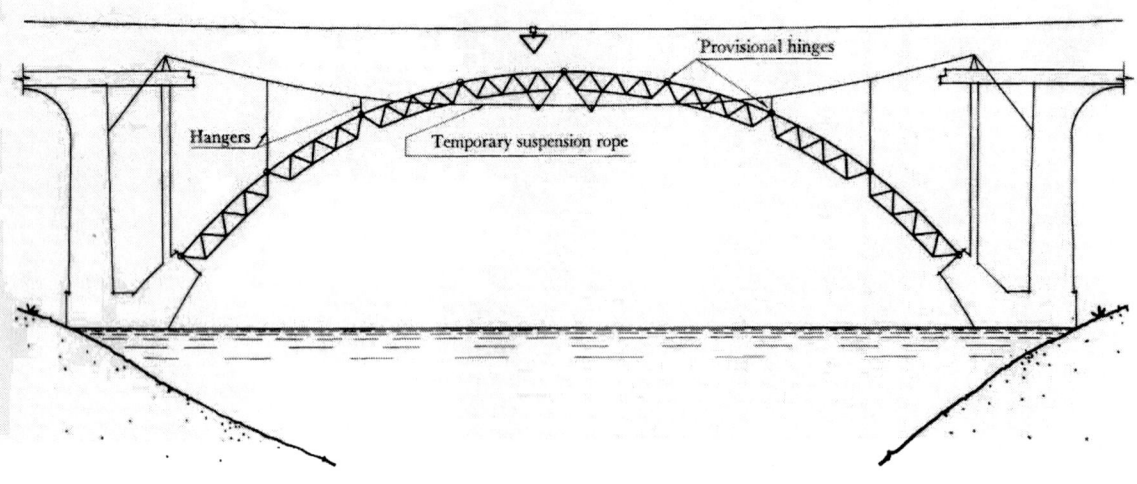

ELEVATION OF CENTERING

TRIANGULAR SECTION OF SIDE GIRDER

The centering consisted of two parallel side girders braced by transverse members, as shown below. Each side girder consisted of a series of steel triangles (above), which were transported and linked to one another with the aid of a hoisting block. Each section of triangles was

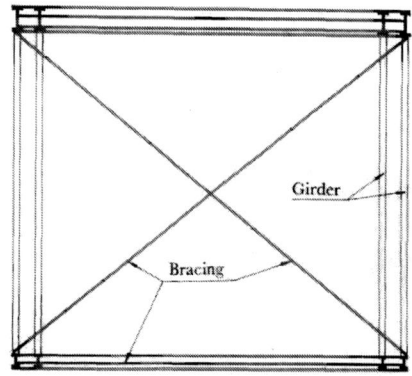

CROSS SECTION OF CENTERING FRAME

Esla Arch 73

then hinged provisionally to the existing structure, and at these hinge points the sections were supported by means of hangers from a suspension cable (see page 72). Once all the triangulated sections of the girder had been hinged together, the position of each hinge was adjusted by means of turnbuckles fitted to the hangers, until the hinged girder had the exact shape required by the design.

When this phase of the erection had been completed, all the joints of the centering were welded on the top chords except the joints at the crown and those at the springing. Thus the centering arch could expand freely under thermal changes without experiencing additional stresses.

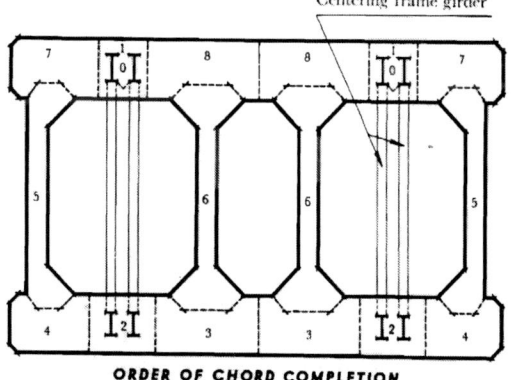

The next stage was to cover the top chords (No. 1, section at right) of the centering arch with a layer of concrete. This operation greatly strengthened the centering.

Then the bottom chords (No. 2) along the intrados of the arch were also embedded in concrete. These chords therefore became suspended, as it were, from the previously hardened top chords by means of the diagonal members.

Centering frame girder

ORDER OF CHORD COMPLETION

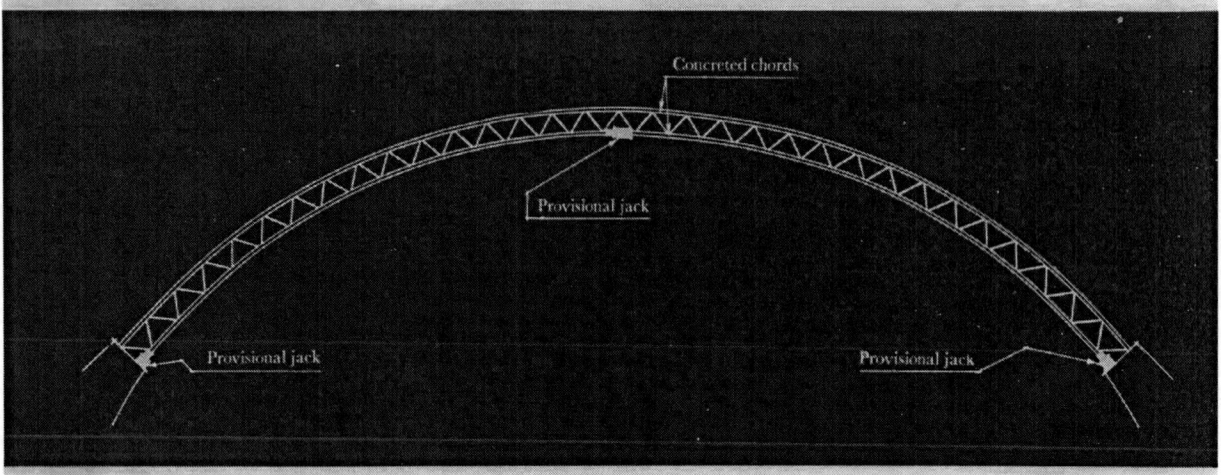

Concreted chords

Provisional jack

Provisional jack

Provisional jack

A set of hydraulic jacks was placed both at the springing and at the crown of the bottom chords as a means of compressing these chords and thereby partly relieving the upper chords from the compression loads that up to this stage had been entirely borne by them. Thus the arch became a continuous, fixed-ended structure instead of a three-hinged arch. There was no harm in this transformation, as both chords of the centering were now covered in thick layers of concrete and were therefore not subject to uneven deformations of any significance. Such deformations were possible as long as one chord was concreted and the other left bare and exposed to the weather.

After this step had been taken, the various chords were concreted one after another until the whole section was complete.

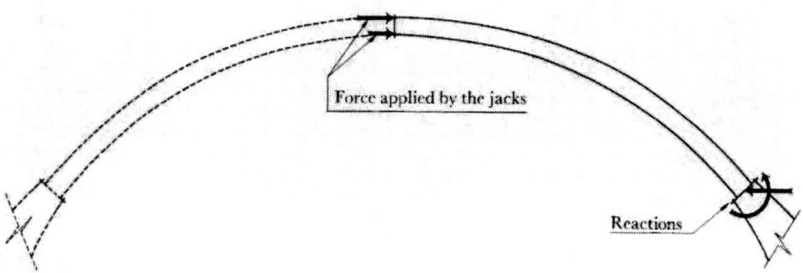

Force applied by the jacks

Reactions

POSITIONING OF BRACING CABLES

It will be noticed, however, that the side girders of the centering had been placed so as to occupy two lateral cavities inside the concrete box section. Had these centering girders been totally embedded with the vertical concrete walls, they might have created sections weak in shear within the concrete because of the considerable inclination of the metal diagonals from the maximum compressive stress directions of the arch.

As the girders had to be placed inside the box cavities, the width of the centering had to be relatively small. As a result, there was a danger of the whole metal frame's becoming laterally unstable under the wind loads and the weight of the first concreted chords.

To avoid this possibility, two anchorage points were fixed along the haunches of the centering frame. These points were fixed in space by means of a set of cables firmly attached to the rocky surroundings and provided with suitable devices for adjusting their load. The anchorage points were attached to vertical slots in the centering frame (as shown

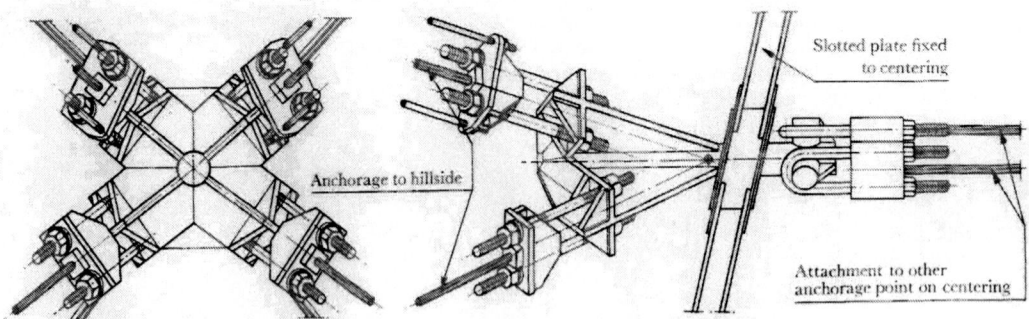

Slotted plate fixed
to centering

Anchorage to hillside

Attachment to other
anchorage point on centering

CABLE DETAILS IN ANCHORAGE DEVICE

above), so that the frame was free to move with respect to the anchorage points in the plane of the arch but not laterally.

As stated previously, the pouring of the concrete of the arch was accomplished along successive longitudinal chords. But furthermore, each chord was concreted sectionally and in a pre-established order so that bending moments on the centering would be minimal. Each section was of such length that it could be concreted in a single operation. Voussoir-shaped free spaces, a few centimeters wide, were left between adjoining sections. These were concreted weeks after the sections had been to give them time to attain most of their shrinkage.

Next followed the operation, usual in the construction of such arches, of opening the crown. With the aid of 36 hydraulic jacks—easily capable of supporting the 7,500-ton thrust of the arch—the crown was opened 3.5 in. This additional space approximately compensated for the shortening of the arch caused by shrinkage and creep under compressive stress.

ANCHORAGE DEVICE

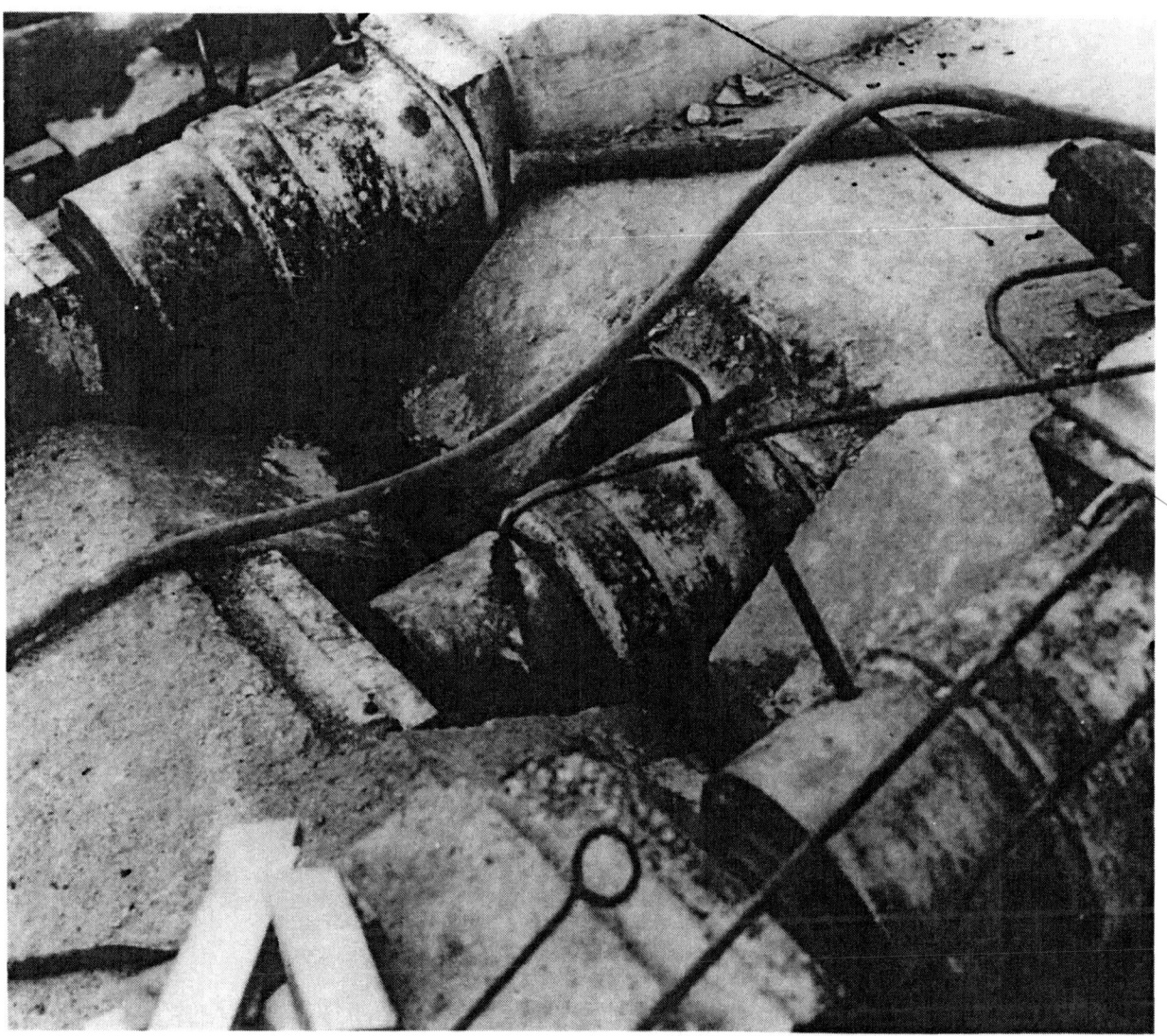

After the crown opening had been concreted along with the empty spaces left by the jacks, the trestlelike spandrel columns and the deck were erected, thus completing the viaduct.

The whole construction process described here met with no difficulties. The anchorage device functioned efficiently, keeping the centering in position even under the most powerful gales. And the measurements and controlled observations to which the arch was continuously subjected showed it to behave perfectly well.

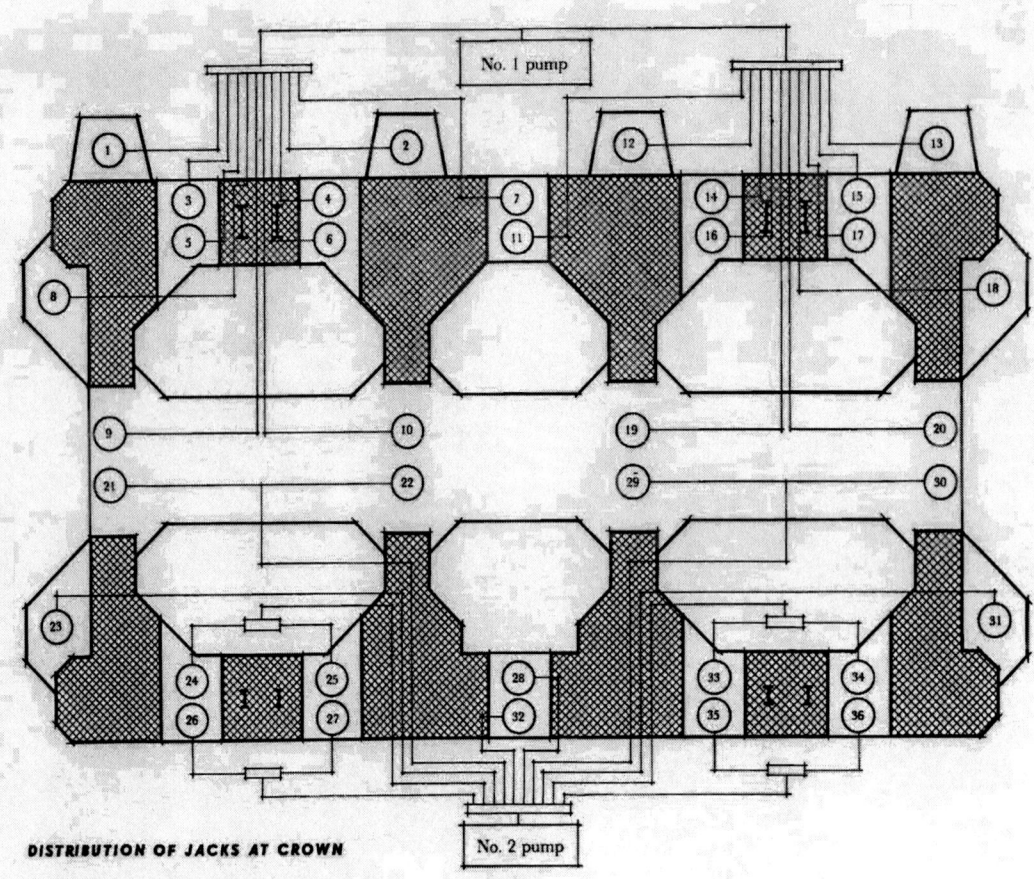

DISTRIBUTION OF JACKS AT CROWN

Nonetheless, the construction procedure was relatively slow, as each concreted strand had to be allowed to harden and shrink before the next was undertaken in order to prevent stress differences from becoming too severe.

Although such local variations in stress cannot be avoided altogether in this type of construction, I suggest that a better method, for other arches of similar size, would be to concrete each chord independently of the others, without inserting transverse joints. Instead, longitudinal joints would be left open between the chords, and these would be prevented from buckling by transverse reinforcements across the joints. With this arrangement, each concreted chord could have its load adjusted separately by jacks applied to it at the crown. And finally the longitudinal joints would be filled in with concrete, thus completing

the arch with optimum stress distribution throughout all its longitudinal strips. As I do not expect to have the opportunity of putting this technique into practice myself, I willingly put it on record here in the hope it may be of some advantage to others.

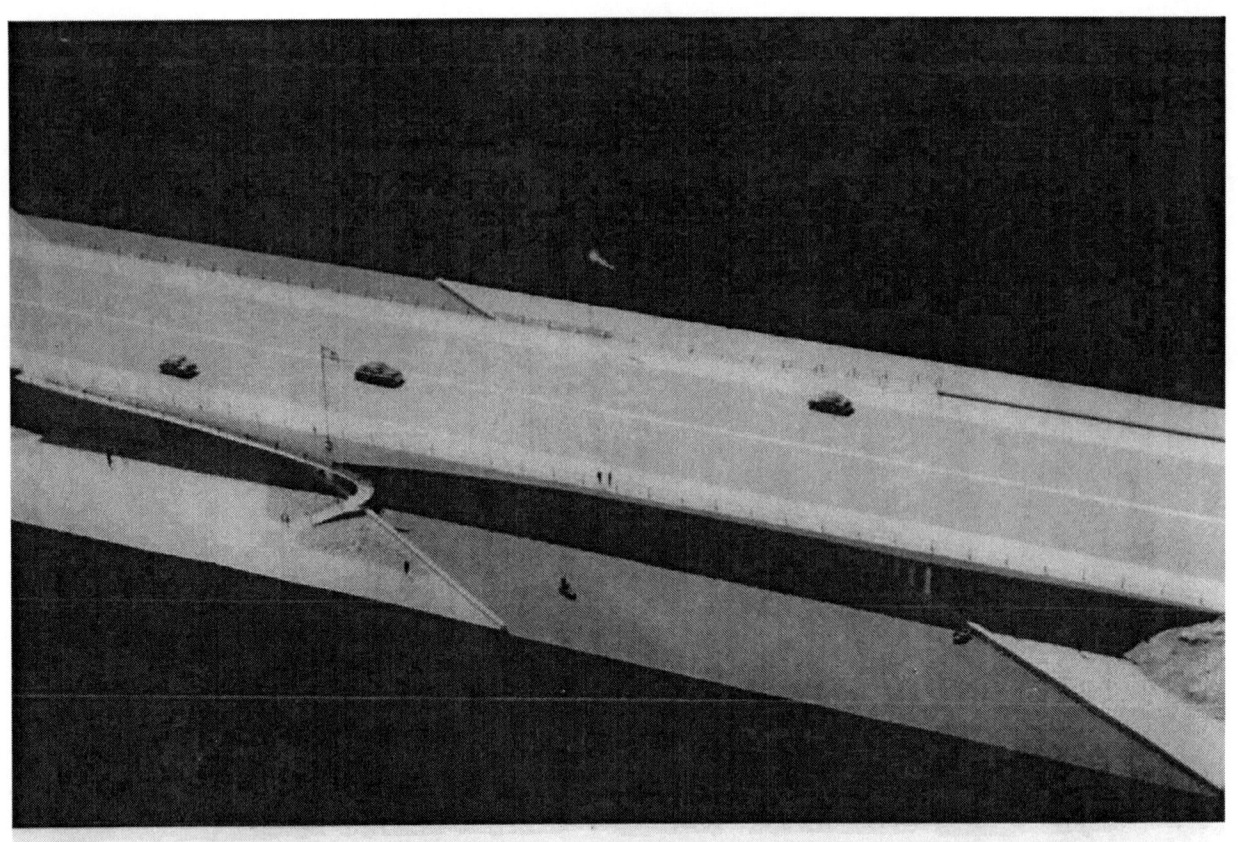

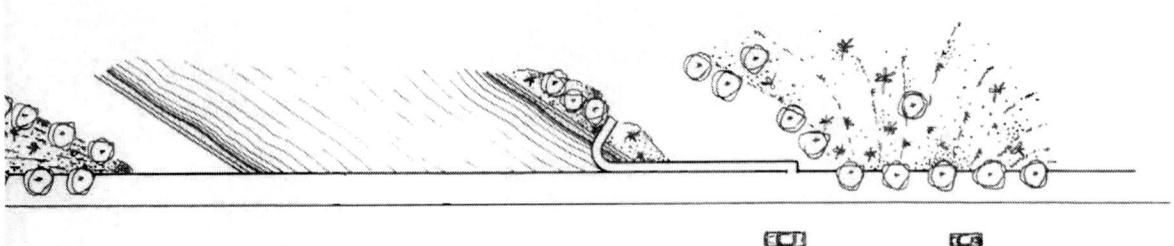

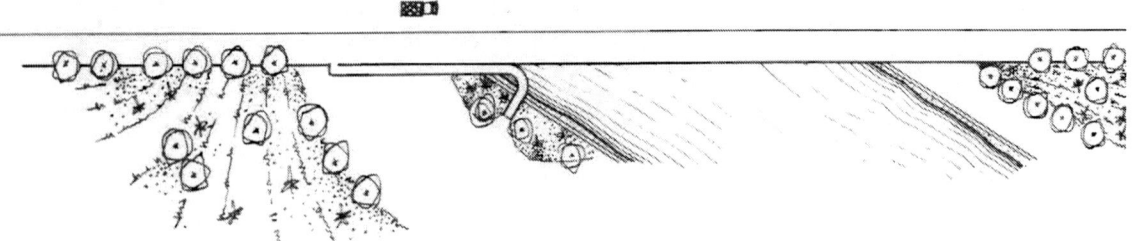

INITIAL PROJECT FOR A SKEW SLAB BRIDGE
1957

This is a bridge of low height running at a very oblique angle. It is formed by a continuous slab of concrete that is post-tensioned in two directions. The overhangs at both ends are anchored into the ground by means of post-tensioned members.

The elevations of the two sides are identical despite the basic asymmetry of the design, that is, the maximum slab depth is on the left side in both views.

The stress distribution was analyzed in a reduced scale model. The thickness of the slab varies in close approximation to the extent of the bending moments at each point.

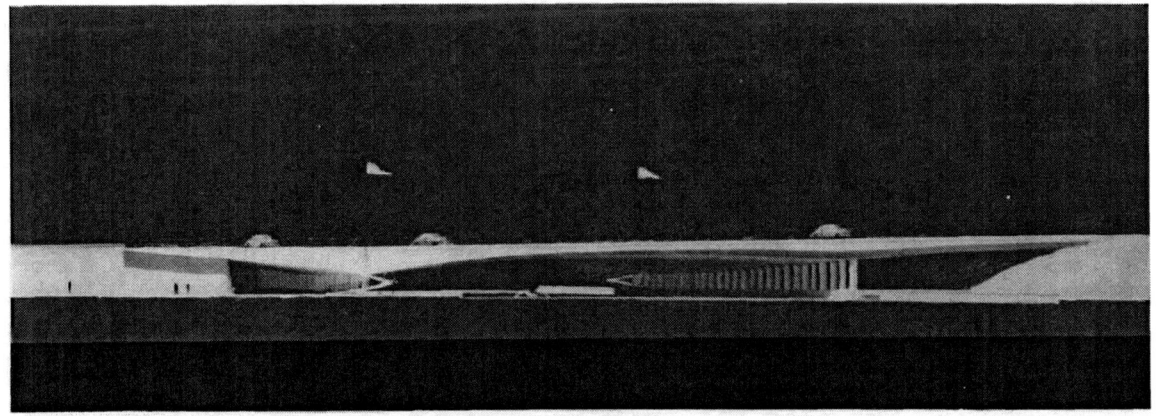

FOUNDATIONS OF SANCTI PETRI BRIDGE
1926

This project involved the construction of a number of caissons to be used in the laying of underwater foundations under compressed air. The caissons were constructed on a hillside and then floated to their operational site, where they were anchored and finally sunk on the sea bed. To obtain a light structure of low draft, a circular design was chosen with a double wall in the shape of hyperboloids of revolution.

This shape has marked advantages. The slightly larger diameter of the lower part of the outer wall reduces the friction generated when the caisson is submerged. The shape of the inner wall prevents the caisson from sinking too rapidly into muddy soils and consequently the danger that the available height of the working chamber, between the soil and the roof, may become too small. Caissons with conventional horizontal ceilings sometimes encounter this difficulty.

Circular, thin-walled cross sections are the most appropriate ones for withstanding hydraulic pressure. The danger of buckling is avoided by two circular ribs—one at the bottom, where the inner and outer walls meet, and the other nearly half way up, where the bracing rods connect the inner funnel to the outer wall, like the spokes of a bicycle wheel. The arrangement of these rods along a conical surface improves their effectiveness, because the hydraulic pressure tends to lower the outer wall with respect to the inner funnel, thus putting the rods in tension.

The walls consist of a simple hollow-brick partition faced on both sides with cement mortar slightly reinforced with wire. Thus the cost of the caisson was very moderate, and the weight also, for the thickness of the wall was not quite 2¾ in. The caisson had a draft of 8 ft, but

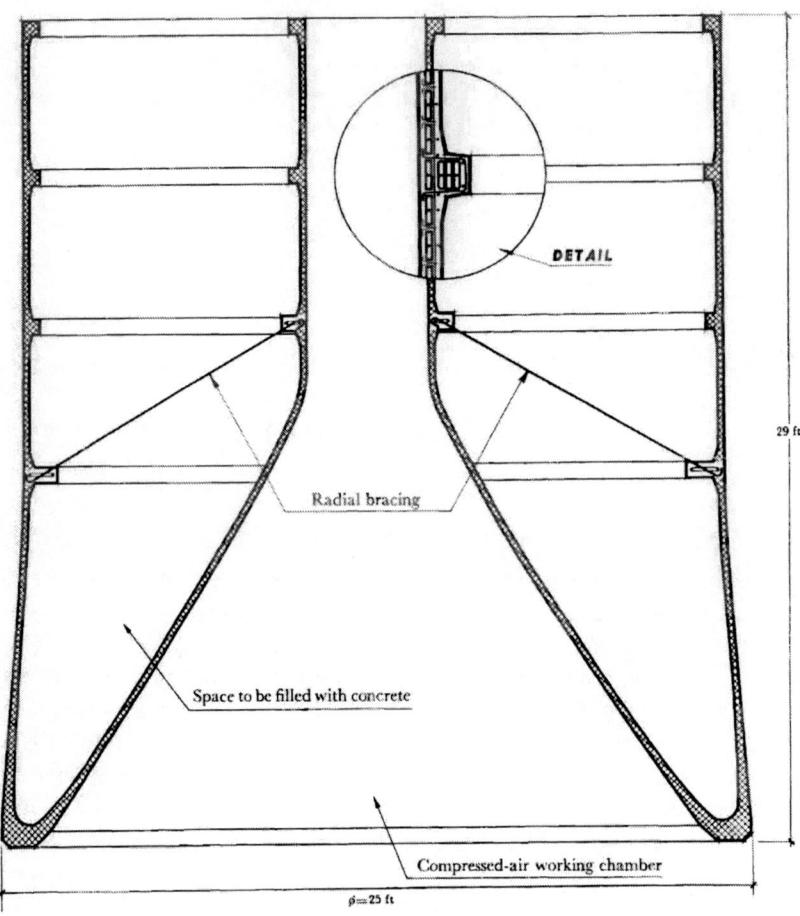

DETAIL

29 ft

Radial bracing

Space to be filled with concrete

Compressed-air working chamber

∅ = 25 ft

for greater ease of handling, it was built on a large timber tub. For the first part of the trip, the caisson was floated in this tub, which had a very low draft. Then the tub was weighted down with ballast until it became separated from the caisson (the tub was recovered later by removing the ballast). The caisson itself was made to sink by placing a concrete fill in the annular space between the two walls (shown above).

The strength of the walls of the caisson was well tested during one of the towing operations. A 200-ton vessel, drifting in a strong gale, hit the caisson sideways with no worse consequence than cutting it adrift and leaving it spinning in the water like a frolicky teetotum—with the author on board.

86   *Viaducts and Aqueducts*

3 SPECIAL STRUCTURES

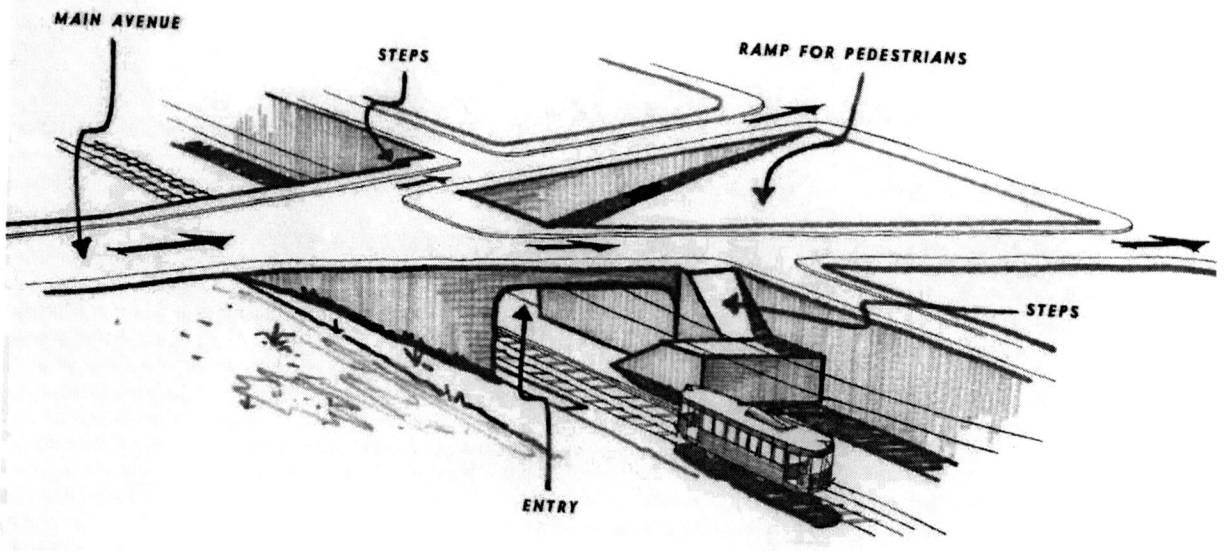

MAIN AVENUE

STEPS

RAMP FOR PEDESTRIANS

STEPS

ENTRY

88

STADIUM STREETCAR STATION
1933

This station was built within the University City of Madrid as a part of its stadium approaches so that the public might have easy access to public transportation. The level of the streetcar track was lower than that of the main avenue leading to the stadium, the two lines of communication crossing each other at right angles. The stairs were to be used by pedestrians from the main avenue who wanted to go either to the stadium or to take the streetcar. The illustration at left provides a functional diagram of the traffic.

The major portion of the station is located in that part of the tunnel below the avenue. Structurally, the tunnel is formed of reinforced concrete portal frames enclosed by a concrete slab, as shown in the diagram on the following page. This slab is attached to the intrados of the frames in some areas and in others to the extrados, according to the character of the bending moments. Consequently, it corresponds everywhere along the frame to the compression chord.

Thus along the central part of the horizontal span where the bending moment is positive, the slab is attached to the outer face of the portal frame. At the rounded corners where the horizontal beams join the vertical columns, and along the top part of the columns, the slab meets the frame on the intrados because the bending moments here are negative. Near the foot of the columns, where the columns are fixed to the base, the slab is again placed on the outside as the bending is again positive.

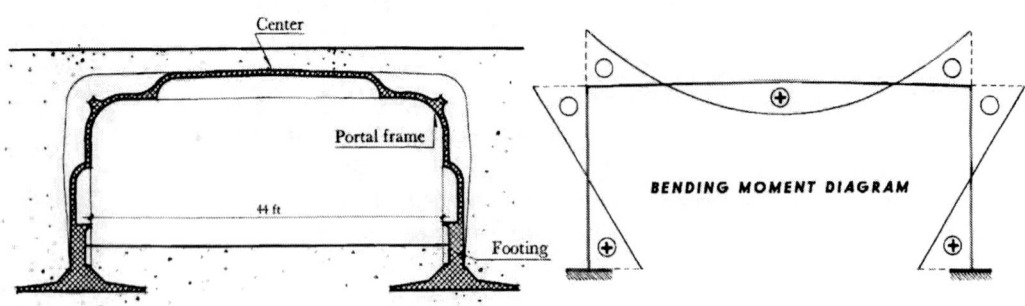

This design gives the station an airier and more pleasant appearance and at the same time creates lateral nooks for a seating ledge along the length of the platform.

In the central portion of the platform, one of the side walls is omitted to provide an entry to the approach ramp. In this area, the portal frames are incomplete and rest on a strong longitudinal beam, which also forms the lintel of the entrance to the platform as well as the balustrade to the deck of the avenue on top.

The concrete is visible throughout, and the only decorative motif is supplied by the marks left in certain areas by the joints of the formwork boards.

Unfortunately, the war interfered with the construction of the stadium, and the urban planning of the zone was altered. In the new planning, this station proved to be superfluous, and the streetcar was diverted elsewhere. Today, the station stands in isolated solitude without hope of being remembered by anyone but its creator, who fondly designed it for the future and even feared that it might prove too small for the crowds that would one day surge through it.

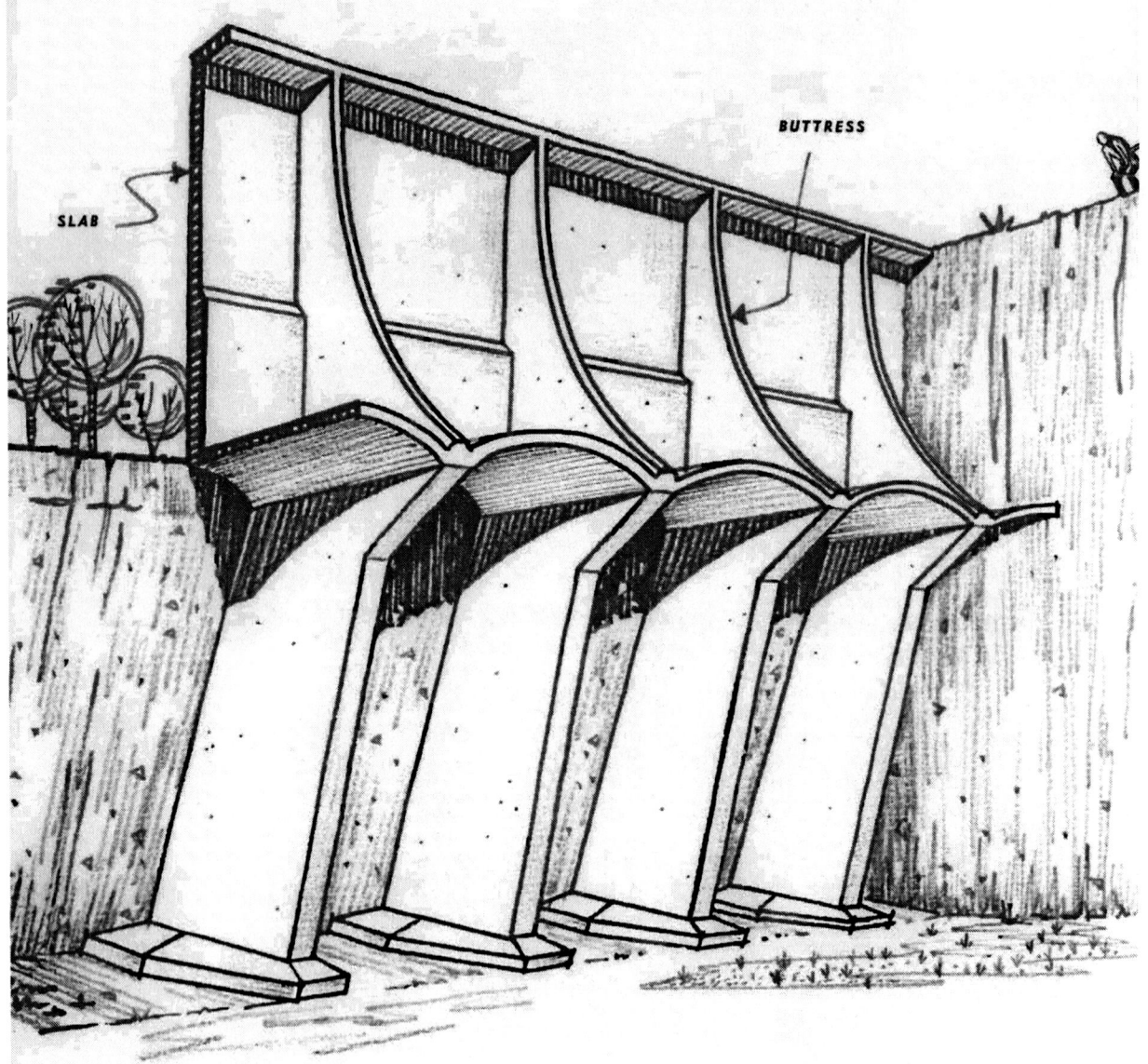

SLAB

BUTTRESS

92

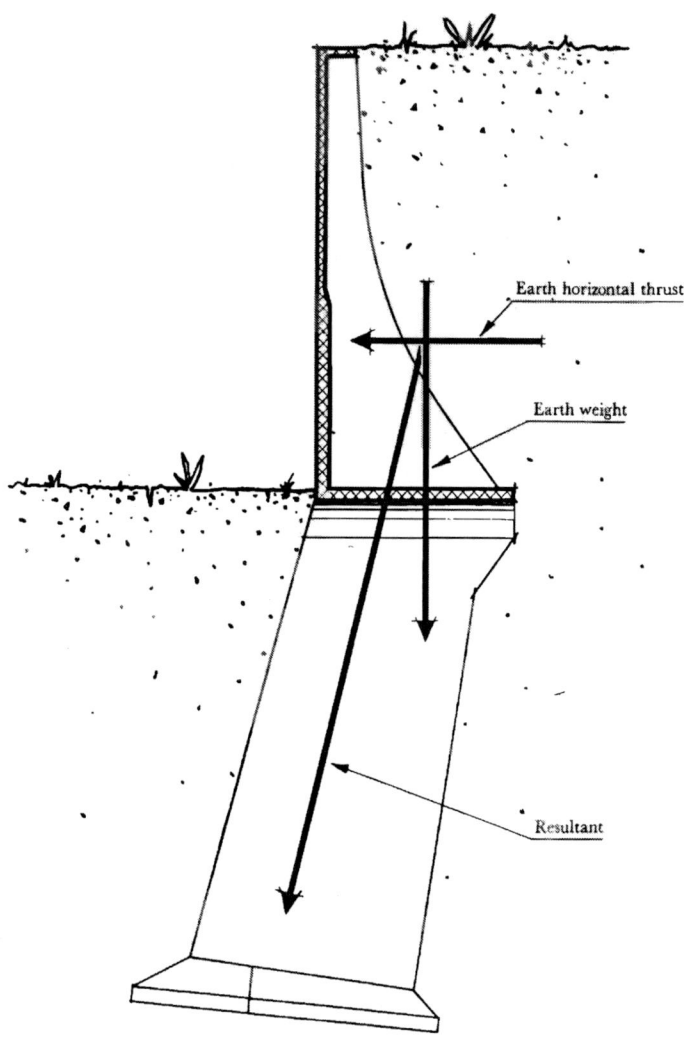

Earth horizontal thrust

Earth weight

Resultant

THE CANTARRANAS RETAINING WALL
1933

The Cantarranas retaining wall in Madrid supports an embankment 36 ft high, with a loose earth fill extending to a depth of 30 ft below the foot of the embankment. The vertical slab that retains the soil is supported by buttresses on the embankment side at 15-ft intervals. The overturning couple caused by the horizontal thrust of the earth fill on the vertical slab is balanced by the downward weight pressing on the horizontal vaults running between the buttresses.

The whole structure rests on reinforced piers that extend down to the foundation footings. These piers are inclined inwards so that the resultant thrust of the retaining wall acts within the area of the footings.

93

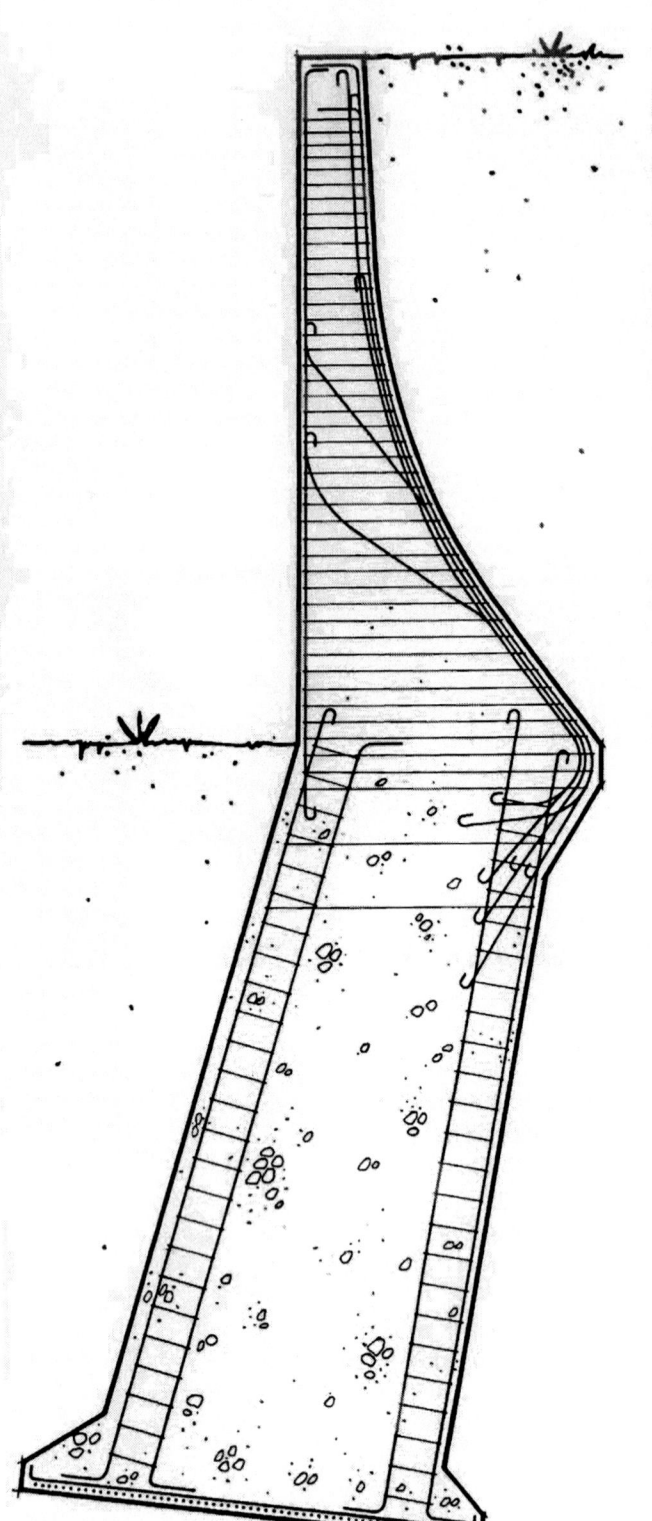

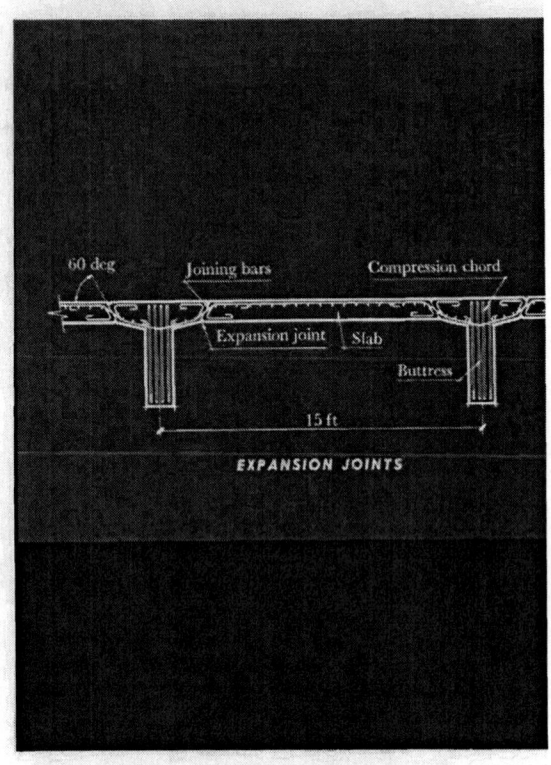

60 deg Joining bars Compression chord

Expansion joint Slab

Buttress

15 ft

EXPANSION JOINTS

BUTTRESS REINFORCEMENT

The vertical slabs are separated vertically by expansion joints, across which the reinforcement rods run continuously. The area of the vertical slab immediately in front of each buttress forms one solid unit with the latter and functions structurally as its compression chord. The buttress itself, fixed at its base and supporting the earth thrust, is functionally a cantilevered beam.

OPERATING AMPHITHEATER   For this project a roof was required that would cover a circular area 70 ft in diameter without intermediate columns. It was also specified that the roof should contain a
circular or polygonal vertical skylight 32 ft in diameter and concentric
with the enclosing ground floor wall.

There were thus two alternatives. The first was to support the skylight windows on cantilevered beams radiating inwards and fixed into
the surrounding structure (see Fig. A). The second method, finally
adopted, was to attach these cantilevered beams rigidly to the central

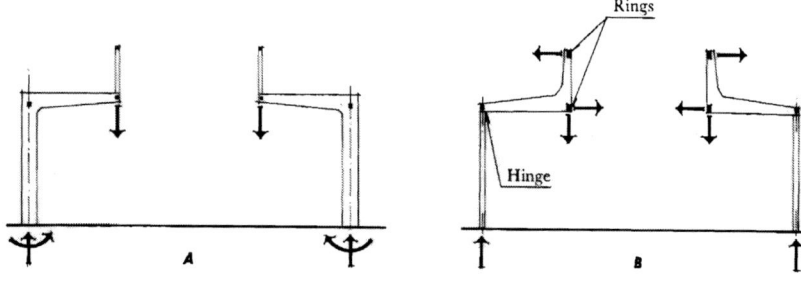

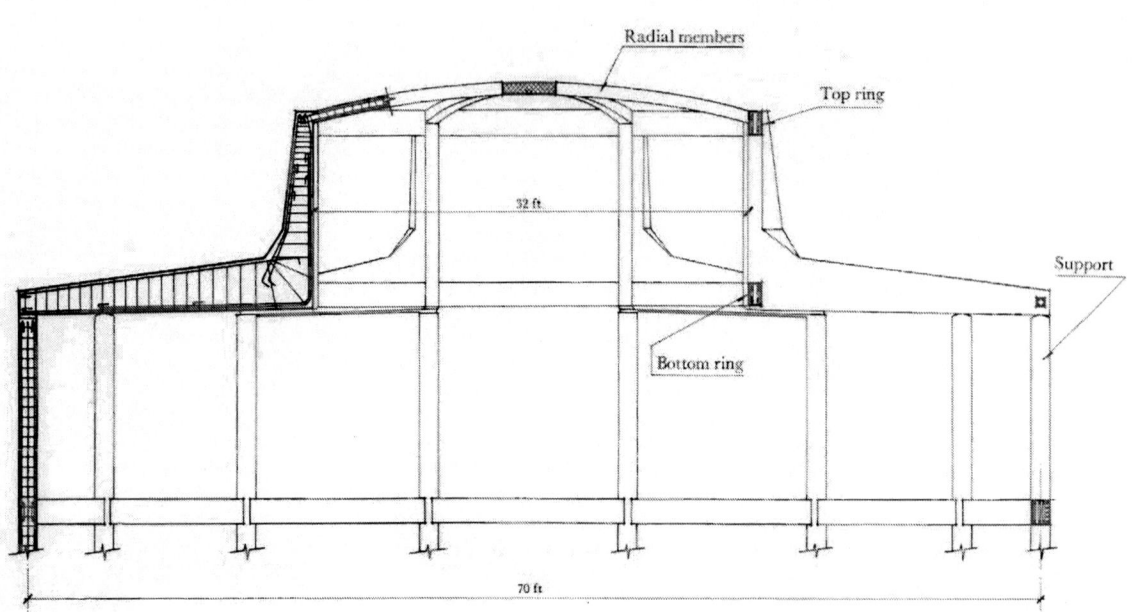

window structure and support them by flexible joints on the peripheral columns (Fig. B). The root bending moment transmitted by these horizontal cantilevers to the vertical members around the skylight is resisted by the couple consisting of the radial components of two loaded polygonal rings, one of which forms the lintel and the other the sill of the skylight. The circular symmetry of the assembly assures these horizontal thrusts of being balanced within each polygonal ring.

The lower polygon is in tension; hence it is in stable equilibrium. The top polygon is in compression, but the danger of buckling is counteracted by the slightly arched radial ribs of the central roof.

As the peripheral columns are subject merely to simple compression and transmit no bending moments to the foundations, their cross section may be small and thus consume the minimum amount of floor space.

The design implies an isostatic structure of a very straightforward calculation as long as the loading remains symmetric about the center. Wind loading, or an uneven vertical load, can upset this symmetry.

With this in mind, the lateral stability of the structure was provided for by the rigidity of the Vierendeel-type closed polygonal girder that is formed by the continuous frame of the skylight. Stresses are calculated by referring all forces to this closed polygonal girder. Although the problem was simplified because of the symmetry of the design, the unsymmetric loading made the structure statically indeterminate, and stress calculation became tedious and approximate. For this reason, theoretical strength estimates were supplemented by the construction of a reduced scale model (above) on which stresses were measured directly.

100   *Special Structures*

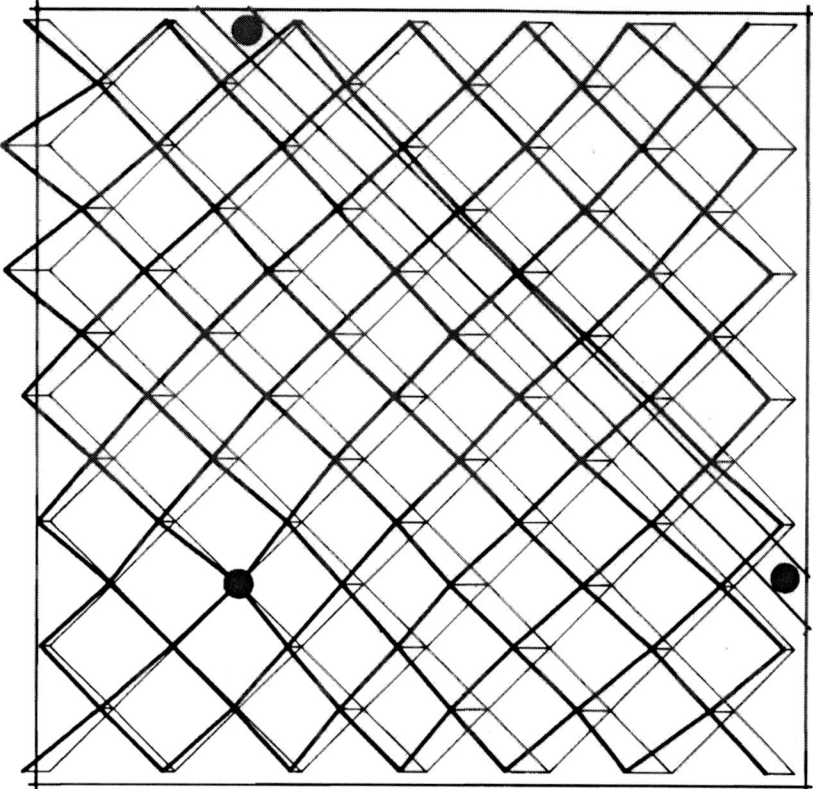

SUN BALCONY SLABS   These rectangular slabs are supported on three points, two of them on beams cantilevered from the facade, the other on a separate column.

As the column is in the open air and runs continuously the whole height of the building (so that its expansions are additive at each floor level), its over-all expansion is different from that of the supports enclosed in the wall masonry. To reduce the effect of this uneven movement of the three points of support, these were freely jointed to the slabs. The diagram above shows how these slabs deflect according to experimental investigation.

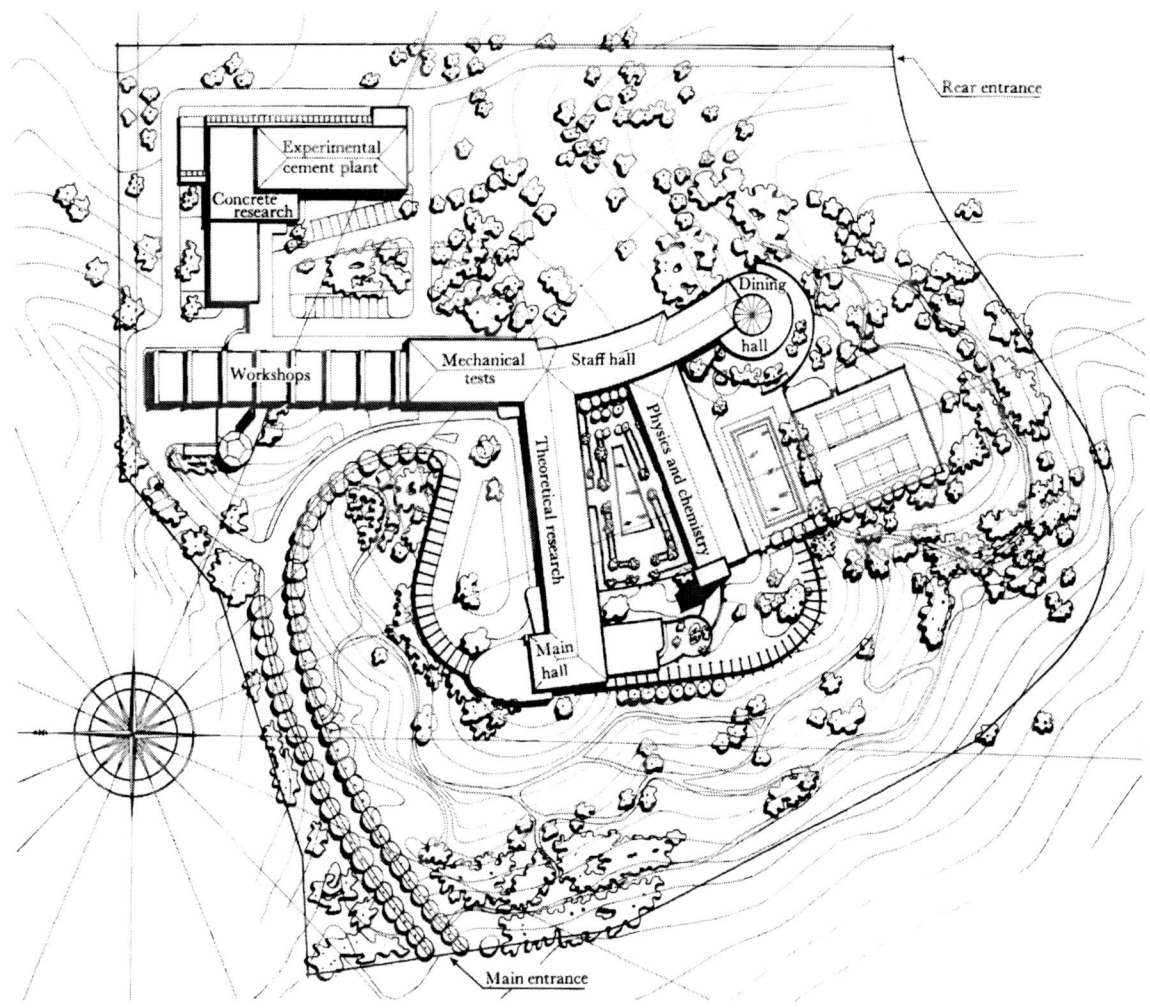

Experimental cement plant

Concrete research

Workshops

Mechanical tests

Staff hall

Theoretical research

Physics and chemistry

Dining hall

Main hall

Rear entrance

Main entrance

COSTILLARES BUILDING
1951

As this book is concerned with the description of structural forms, it goes beyond our purpose to comment at length on this set of buildings. Their general layout depends on the functional requirements of the research institute that they house and on the topographical features of the ground where they stand. We shall limit ourselves, therefore, to a brief reference to certain novel structural aspects of the project.

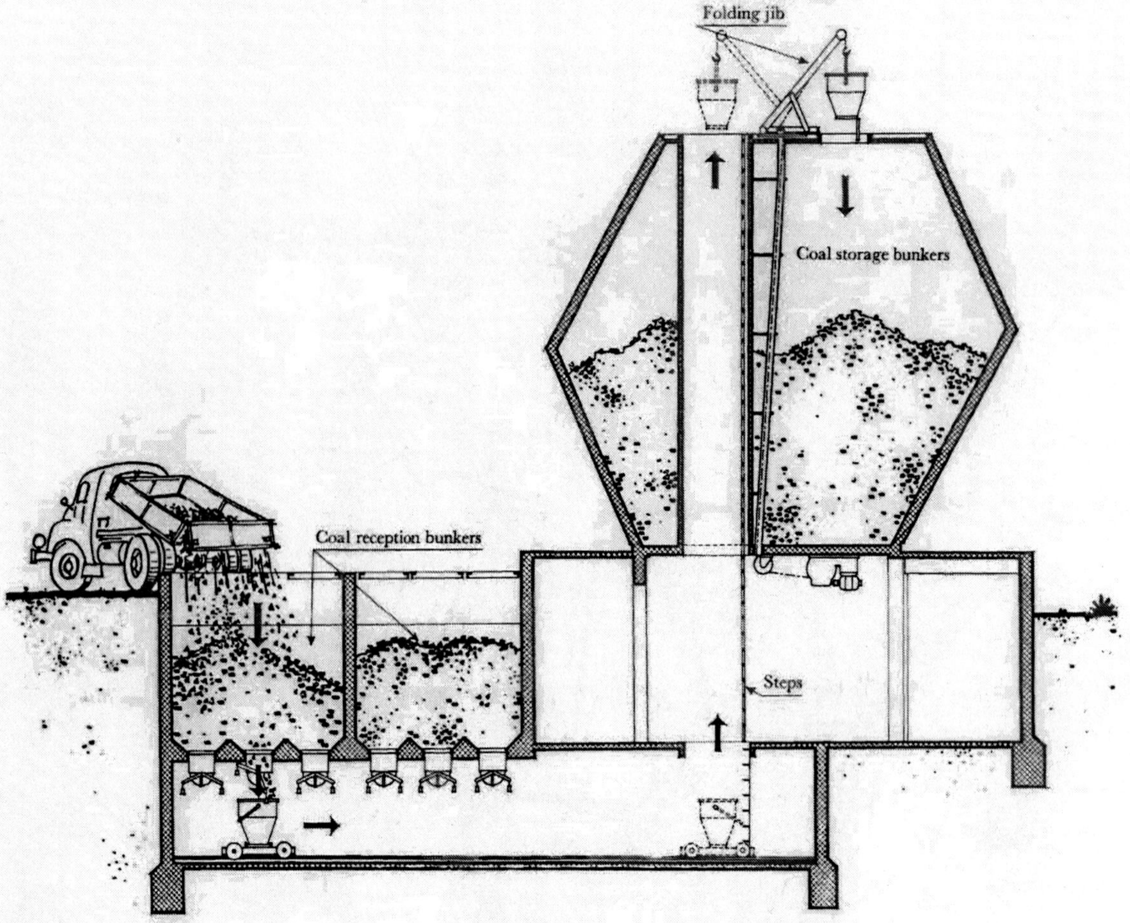

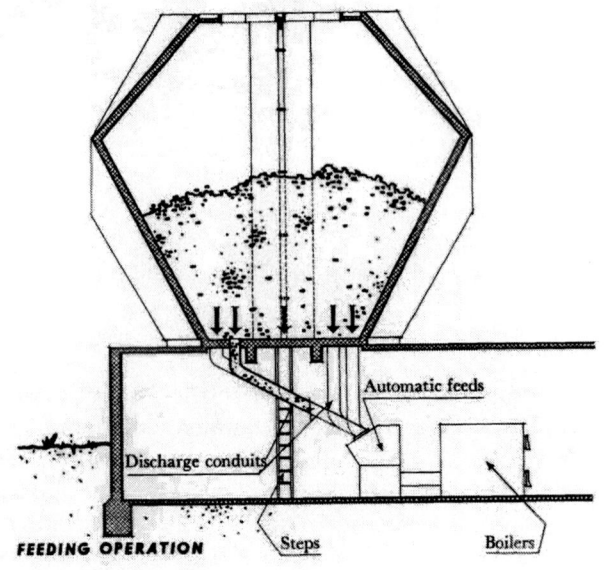

Folding jib

Coal storage bunkers

Coal reception bunkers

Steps

STORAGE OPERATION

Automatic feeds

Discharge conduits

Steps

Boilers

FEEDING OPERATION

DODECAHEDRAL COAL SILO   One of these novel constructions is the coal silo. Made of reinforced concrete, it is located over the boiler room and is shaped like a great dodecahedron. Its height is 26 ft. An interior lift elevates the coal from the trolleys, which have transported it from the hoppers, where it had originally been discharged from the trucks. The bottom of the dodecahedron has openings leading directly to the automatic feeding mechanism of the boilers. (See diagrams at left.)

The sphere provides the best volume-surface ratio for such structures, but that of the dodecahedron is nearly as good. Furthermore, the dodecahedron is easier to build and has considerable aesthetic and decorative value. For these reasons, it was adopted in preference to any other alternative.

CIRCULAR DINING HALL   Another unusual form is that of the circular dining hall. Its roof rests on a circular row of columns from which it cantilevers outwards to the rim. Here curved glass sliding doors can rotate back to leave a 180-deg clear opening. The dining hall thus merges, without discontinuity, into open air (provided the weather is suitably clement).

It was first thought to construct this roof as a conical reinforced concrete thin shell or membrane (elevation shown at upper right). But the cost of the formwork made that design impracticable.

The roof was finally built on a structure of radiating metal cantilevered girders, each of them resting on one of the columns.

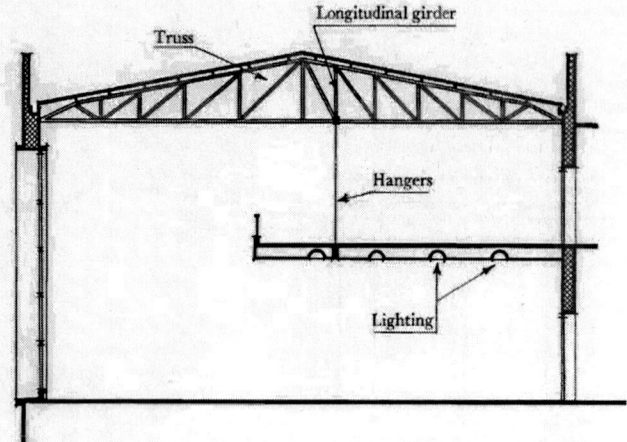

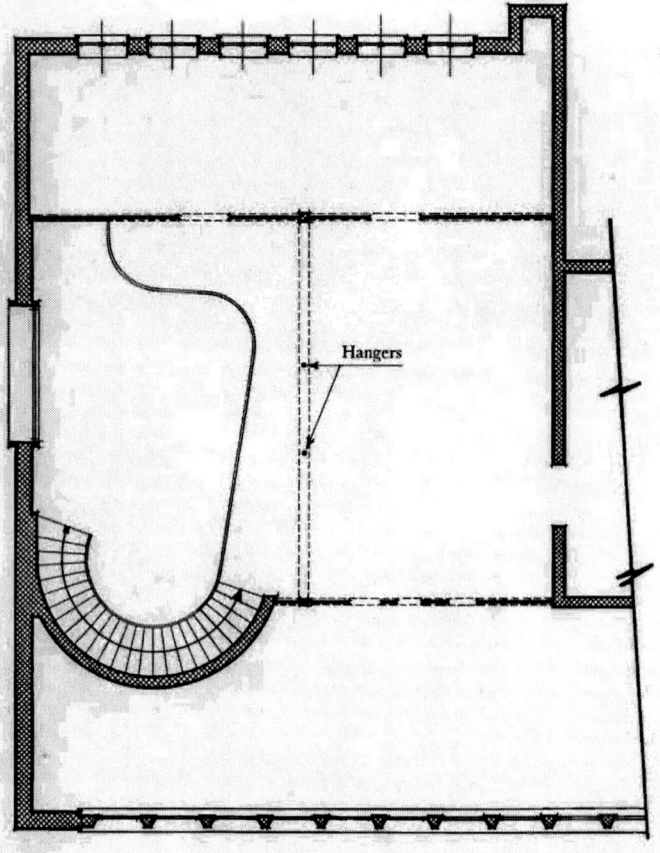

Mention might also be made, in the way of structural curiosity, of the arrangement for a second floor level within the main hall. A plan for this floor level would ordinarily call either for columns, breaking up the continuity of the lower floor, or else for beams of considerable depth and unsightly effect. To overcome these drawbacks, the balcony was suspended by means of two thin hangers from the roof structure (the roof consists of triangular trusses of sufficiently ample proportions to support a supplementary load economically). This solution, though rational and cheap, is something of a trick. But precisely for that reason it has the merit of amusing the waiting visitor, whose mind is intrigued by the apparent lack of support of such a shallow long-span balcony.

The elements of the pergola over the peripheral pathway shown on the opposite page are Bernoullian lemniscates with zero end curvature. The mesh has a more or less hyperbolic-paraboloid shape.

DEFLECTION DIAGRAM OF HYDROSTATIC PRESSURE

110

THE CAÑELLES DAM
1956

This dam, 460 ft high, is presently under construction near Lérida. Although not original in appearance, it is of interest in that it was the object of a detailed preliminary study involving 17 different reduced scale models (one shown above) before the final design was reached. The results of the tests on one model determined the modifications to be introduced in the next, the altered form of which was again subjected to experimental investigation.

The initial models were made of an easily moldable material with no appreciable tensile strength but a compressive strength equivalent to 700 psi in the actual dam. Their sole purpose was to indicate whether the projected dam would be strong enough to support both its own weight and the hydrostatic pressure of the water (see sketch at left).

Succeeding models were made of another material by means of which it was possible to determine the isostatic pattern (directions of principal stresses) on both faces of the dam. The actual stresses were later measured by means of strain gages, and the margin of error was found to be less than 30 psi.

The investigation was regarded as complete when a dam shape was developed with a maximum compressive stress of 700 psi and negligible tensile stress on the upstream face. The resulting form has variable curvature both vertically and horizontally. The curvature of the horizontal arches diminishes from the crown to the springing, where the greater rigidity of the vertical cantilevers relieves the pressure over the arches. The materials for the models, which were specially developed to meet the requirements of each type of research, were such that the model of the dam and of the supporting soil had the same relative moduli of elasticity as the actual dam and rock foundation. The elastic properties of the rock foundation had been previously ascertained.

A check on the strength of the dam by the well known trial-load method showed the advantages of the experimental procedure adopted.

A similar technique employing the same kind of materials has been successfully employed in the stress calculation of various shells and laminar shapes to which analytical methods are not easily applicable. It is a technique that gives the designer a great freedom in the choice of shell forms.

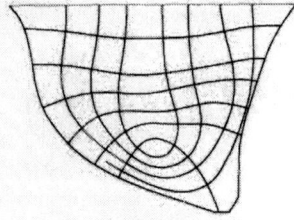

DOWNSTREAM STRESS PATTERN

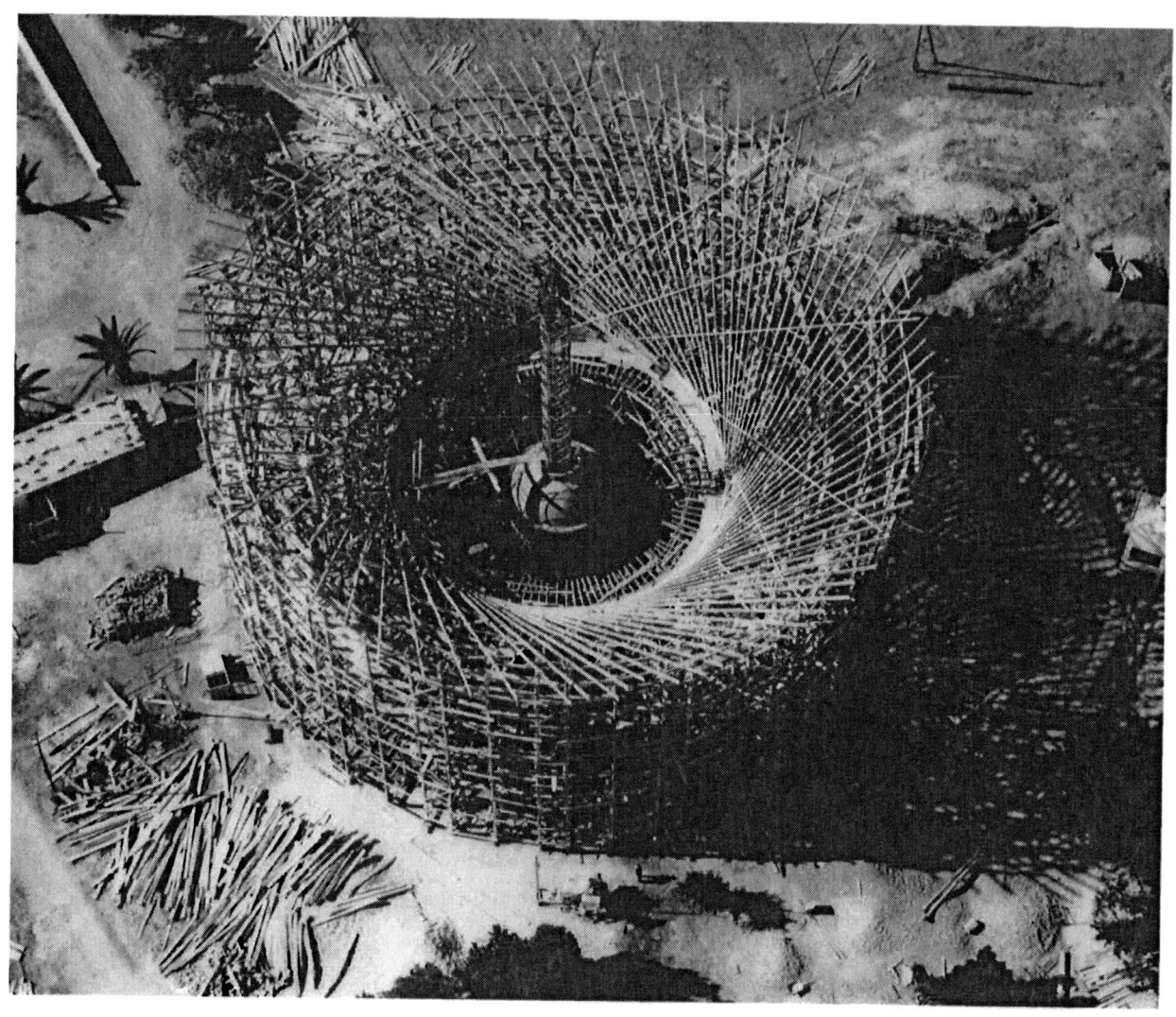

WATER TANK AT FEDALA
1956

The main problem in designing this tank (925,000-gal capacity) was finding a satisfactory method of water-proofing. As a result, the initial shape—a truncated cone—was changed to that of a hyperboloid of revolution, which was post-tensioned along the two families of straight lines typical of the hyperboloid. Simultaneous compression along the generators and directrixes was thereby achieved and the danger of fissuration avoided.

113

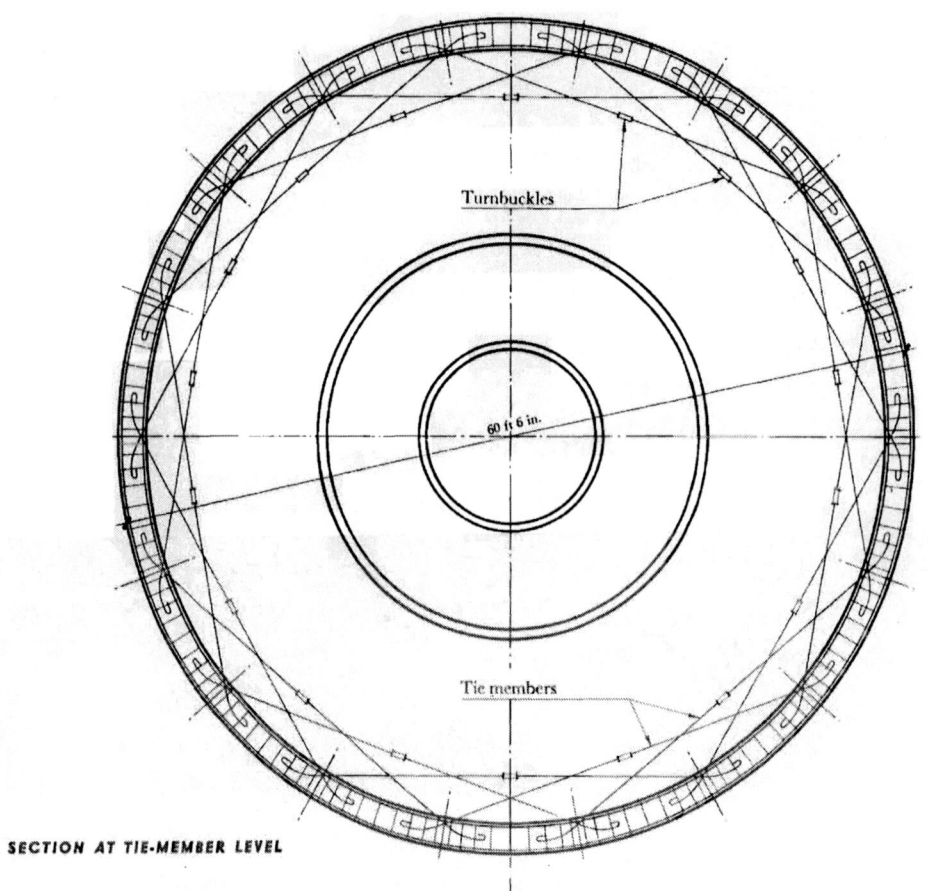

Turnbuckles

60 ft 6 in.

Tie members

HORIZONTAL SECTION AT TIE-MEMBER LEVEL

The bottom of the tank consists of an annular vault of reinforced concrete. The top of the tank, which it supports, is an annular vault made of hollow brick. To avoid circumferential tensile stresses in the concrete vault, the outer ring is post-tensioned by means of members forming a star-shaped polygon. This arrangement leaves room in the center of the tank for the central part of the supporting vault.

The roof consists of toric vaults of three layers of hollow brick placed on radially disposed concrete joists.

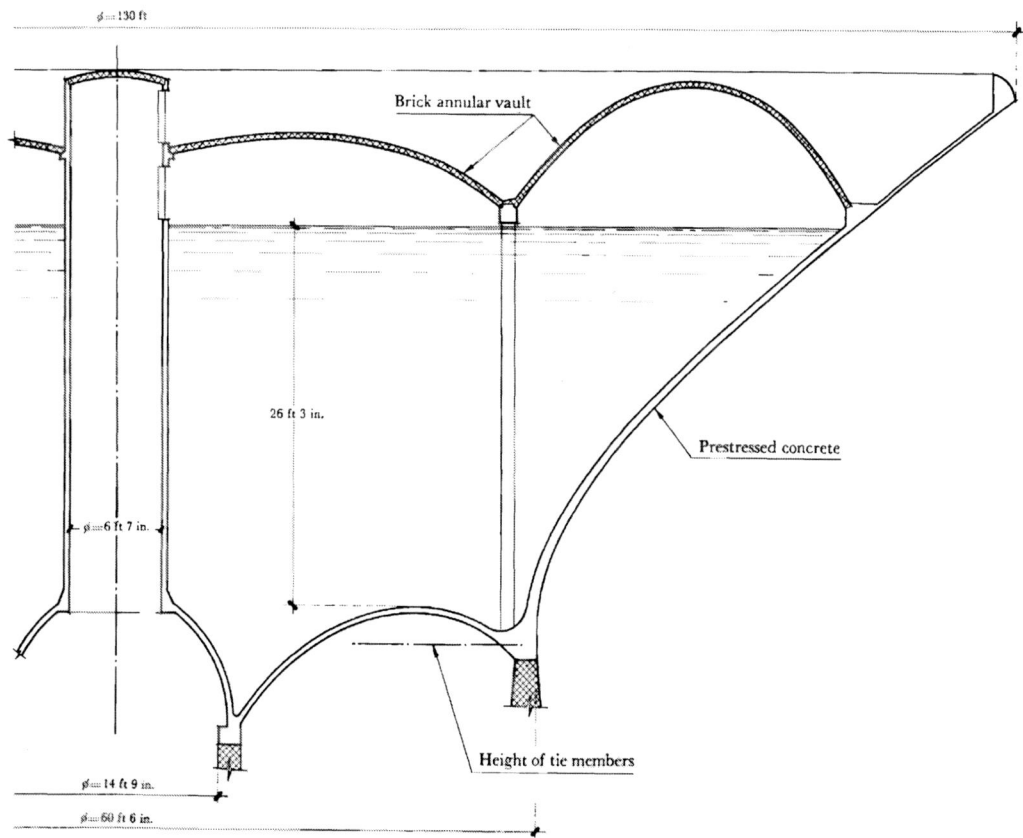

ϕ = 130 ft

Brick annular vault

26 ft 3 in.

Prestressed concrete

ϕ = 6 ft 7 in.

Height of tie members

ϕ = 14 ft 9 in.

ϕ = 60 ft 6 in.

A DIFFERENT SOLUTION OF A SIMILAR PROBLEM
1957

As in previous water works projects, the basic design aim for this tank (264,000-gal capacity) was to avoid, at low cost, the existence of tensile stresses in the face that is in contact with the water.

To this end, the wall—in the approximate shape of a truncated cone—is provided with six radial hinges along six generator lines. The circumferential reinforcement runs near the external face. At time of concreting, the horizontal sections consist of six arcs of a circle with a slightly larger radius (see Fig. A) than that of the corresponding inscribed circumference (Fig. B). The radius of these sectors is designed to deflect sufficiently under the water pressure for the internal face to be under compression. The grooves at the hinges are first filled with gravel and afterwards injected with special cement.

This operation of deforming the shell to compress its inner face can also be carried out before water pressure is applied. Jacks can be used to force the grooves of the hinges to open a bit, and these grooves can be concreted later. The concreted joints will then be in compression, provided the opening made by the jacks is slightly greater than that which the water pressure would produce later.

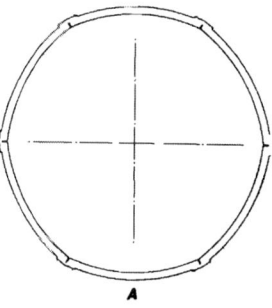

A

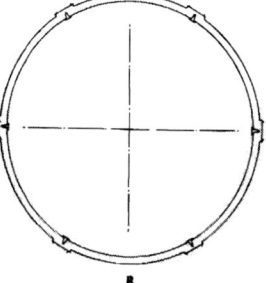

B

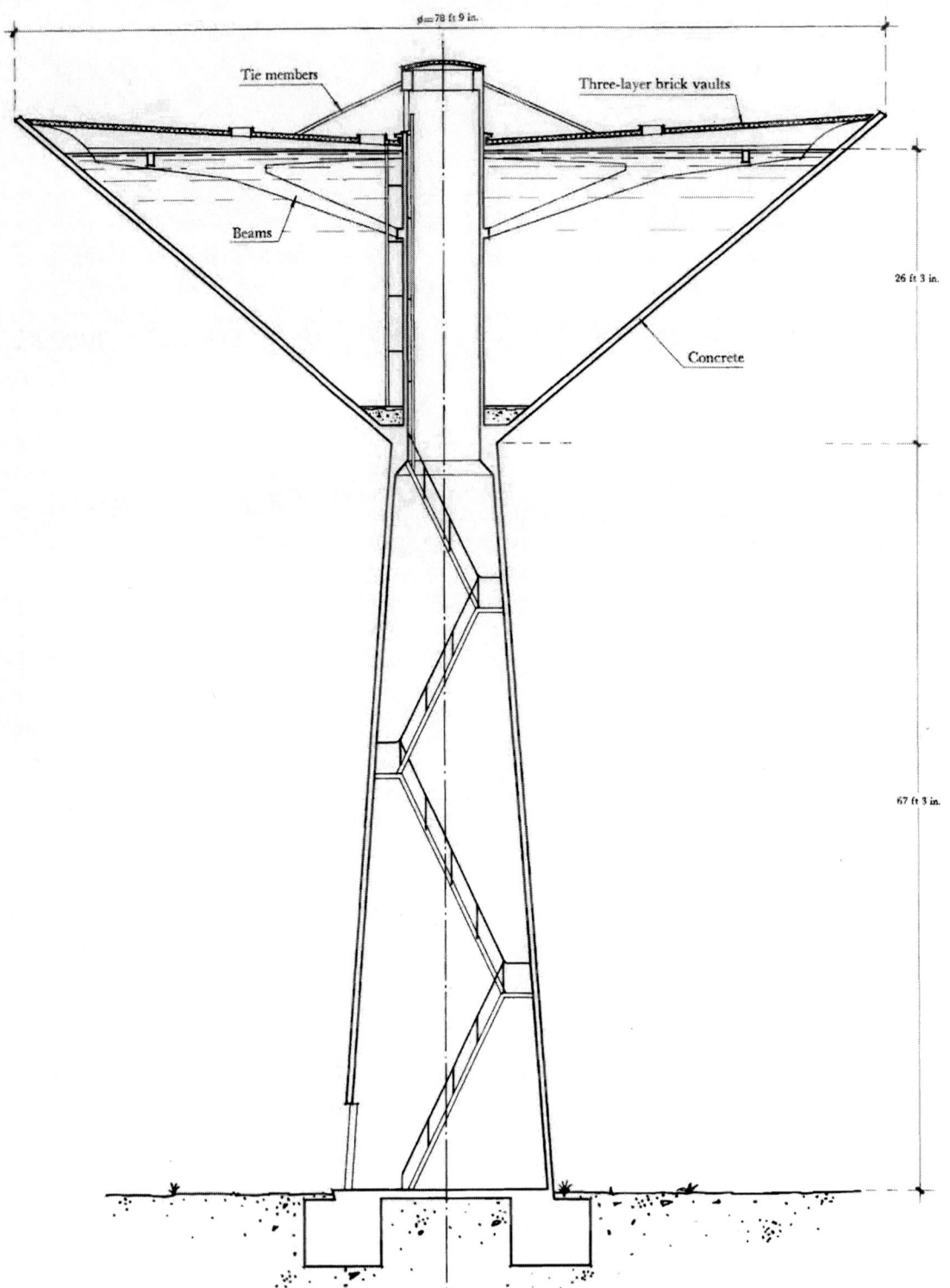

Tie members

Three-layer brick vaults

Beams

Concrete

ø=78 ft 9 in.

26 ft 3 in.

67 ft 3 in.

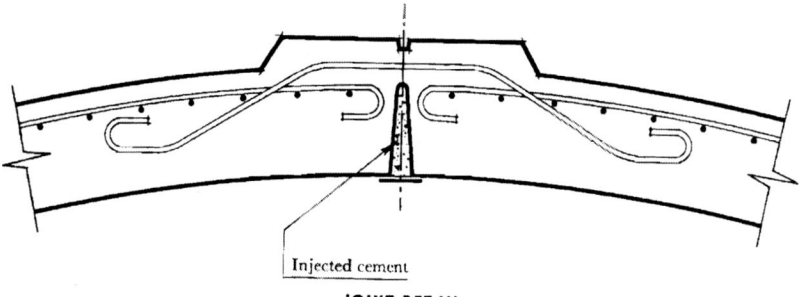

Injected cement

JOINT DETAIL

There is no tendency for tensile stresses to develop along the generators, and the weight of the wall is enough to provide a slight compression that increases in the downward direction proportionally to the
water pressure. Poisson's effect adds to this compression as a result of
the circumferential internal compression of the wall.

4 STEEL AND COMPOSITE STRUCTURES

HANGAR AT CUATRO VIENTOS

HANGARS AT TORREJON AND BARAJAS

TRIANGULATED SHELL ROOFS

LAS CORTS FOOTBALL STADIUM

COMPOSITE STEEL AND REINFORCED
CONCRETE BRIDGES

HANGAR AT CUATRO VIENTOS
1949

The roof stringers of this hangar rest on metal arches of 115-ft span. The arches cross each other diagonally so that the assembly forms a vaulted reticule of great rigidity well able to withstand the wind forces acting on the vertical projections of the hangar.

The arches bear on cantilevered beams that jut beyond the lateral portal frames, but none of these frames have to withstand the side thrust of the arches except the two at each end. Braced by diagonal members of the necessary strength, these end frames are able to take the total side thrust of the whole arched structure, including the main longitudinal stringers. Consequently, each of the two halves of the roof structure functions like an inclined girder (leaning longitudinally against its twin) of great strength and rigidity although very light in weight.

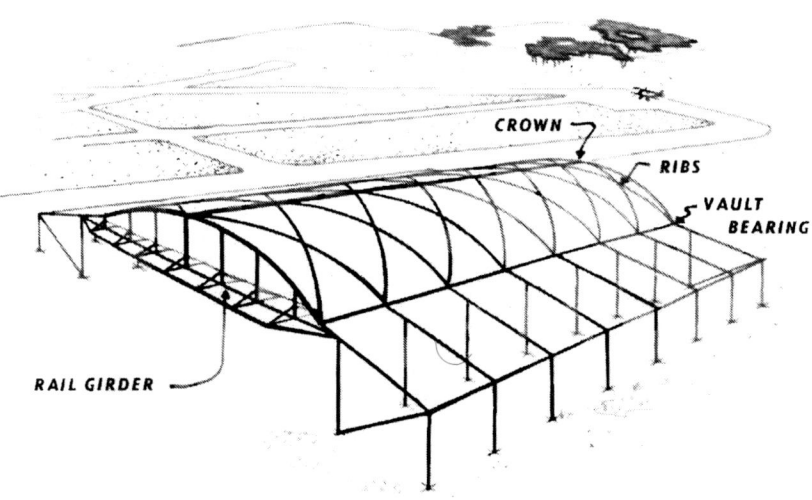

The arches were assembled on the ground with the aid of provisional tie members. The assembly was then lifted to its final location and suspended from the cantilevers of the lateral portal frames. After the arches had been hinged to their supports, the tie members were removed. To have left these members in place would only have interfered

with the otherwise unobstructed spaciousness of the interior and would
have required sliding bearings at the springing to cope with their
thermal expansions and contractions.

The facing arch supports the rail girder on which the doors slide.
This girder must withstand the horizontal wind pressure acting on the
door surfaces.

The attachments of this girder to the springing of the facing arch are
designed to allow for the free expansion of the girders without hinder-
ing the transmission of horizontal wind thrust to the longitudinal
stringers. These loads are eventually resisted by suitably buttressed
walls at the rear side of the hangar.

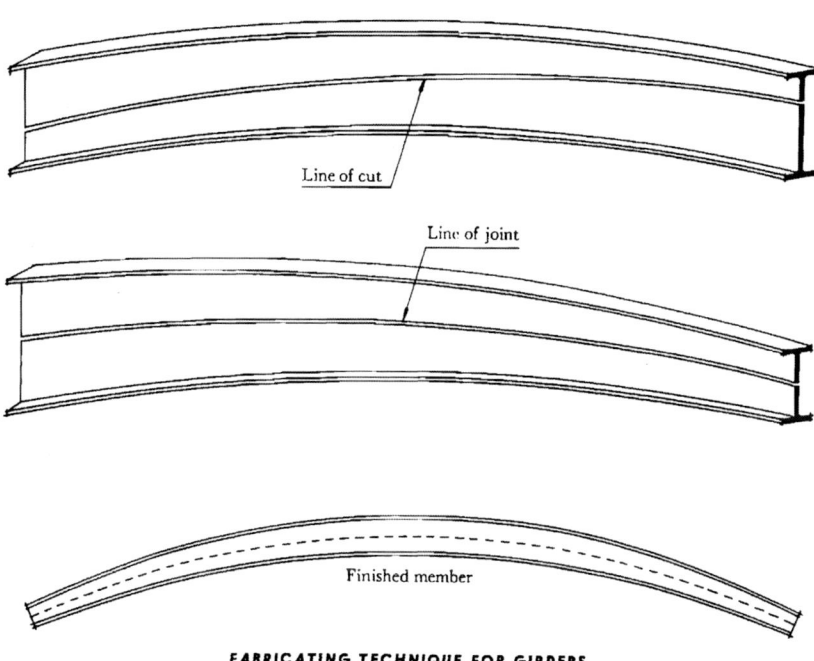

FABRICATING TECHNIQUE FOR GIRDERS

As the arches are three-hinged, the most severe bending moment
occurs at the haunches. Accordingly, the depth of the arches begins to
increase at the springing, reaches its maximum at the quarter-span, and
is again smallest at the crown. The fabrication of full web girders with
this variation in depth is easily and inexpensively accomplished by cutting the web of the girder diagonally and then welding the two parts,
having turned one of them around.

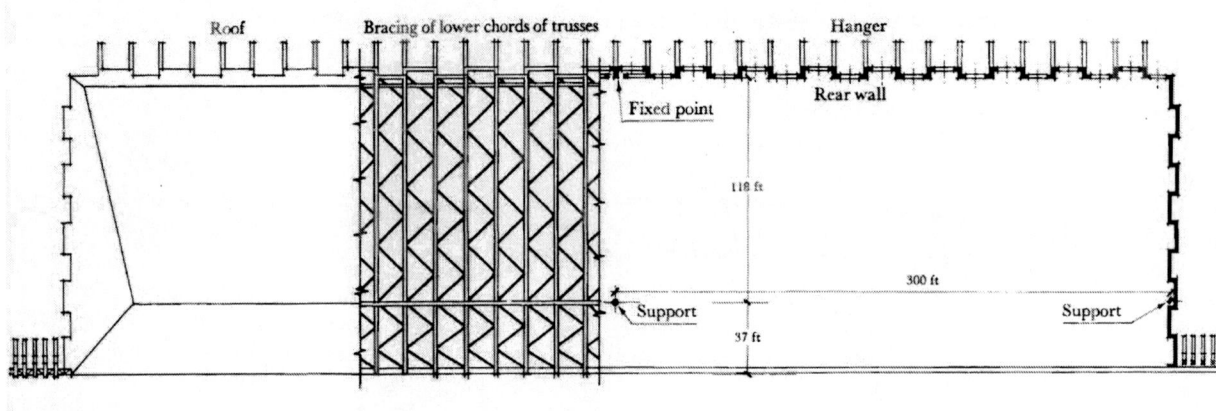

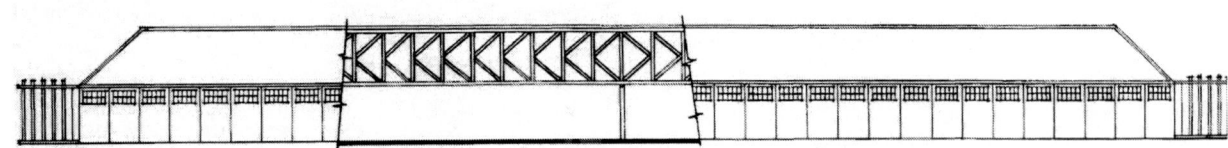

GENERAL ELEVATION AND SECTIONS

126

HANGARS AT TORREJON AND BARAJAS
1942-1945

The functional requirements for both these hangars were that they should enclose a rectangular surface of 600 x 155 ft, with one longitudinal side left open to be fitted with sliding doors. This side was to have only one intermediate support, which was to be recessed no more than 33 ft from the doors. The loading conditions for the roof structure included its own weight, a snow loading of 13.5 psf, and windage.

To reduce the wind pressure on the lateral walls as much as possible, the roof was to be sloped down to the minimum specified height (for the Torrejon hangar) of 30 ft along the four sides. On the other hand, the slope of the roof had to be the minimum compatible with the requirement that rain be prevented from penetrating the joints of the asbestos cement sheeting.

TORREJON CROSS SECTION

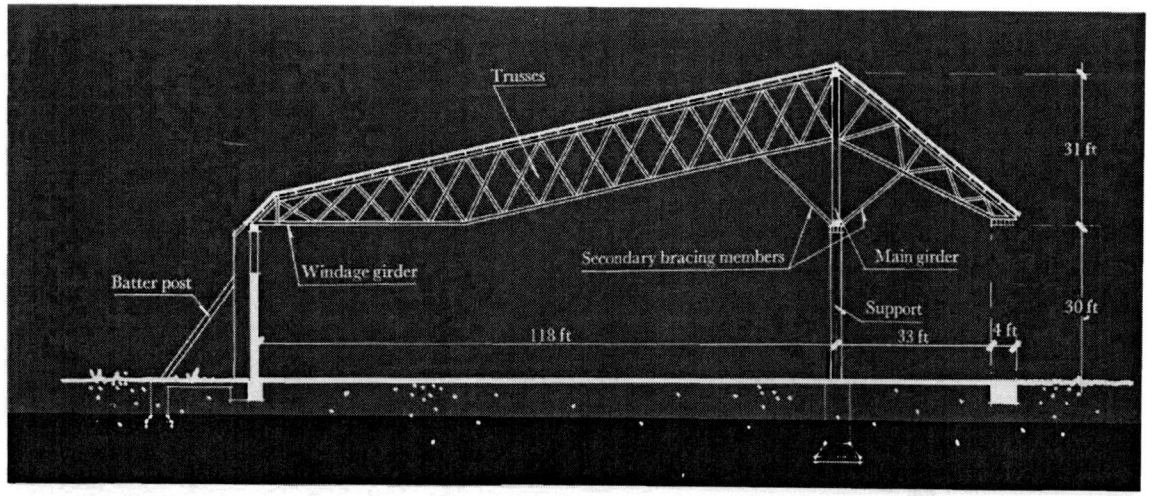

The best way of meeting these specifications was to place a longitudinal girder parallel to the open side of the hangar at a distance of 33 ft from the sliding doors, and to rest the transverse trussed girder upon it. These girders in turn would support the roof. The total height of the longitudinal girder was therefore limited by the rear roof slope of 13 deg.

This main longitudinal girder is continuous over two spans, each 300 ft long. It rests on three supports, one at the center of the girder and the other two lodged in the lateral walls. The transverse trussed girders are supported on the rear wall and on the longitudinal girder, with a free overhang reaching up to the plane of the sliding doors.

The height of the main girder worked out to be 31 ft. But it would have been uneconomical to make the transverse trussed girders of this height also. Their chords would have been the lighter for it, but the

longer diagonals would have required larger sections to avoid buckling. Hence these trussed girders were made 14 ft deep and linked up with the intermediate nodes of the K-shaped bracing of the main girder.

The bars connecting the trussed girders to the lower chord of the main girder are only secondary bracing members. They counteract the tendency of the chord to buckle near the central support where the chord is in compression.

The transverse trussed girders have an X-type bracing, that is, the diagonals cross each other at their midpoints. This design was chosen to reduce by one half the free length of these members and to improve their stability in the plane of the truss. In the direction normal to this plane, it sufficed to attach each pair of extruded sections (making up each diagonal) by means of gusset plates, so that the moment of inertia of the diagonal as a whole was greatly increased.

A K-type triangulation was adopted for the main girder. This design not only reduces secondary stresses considerably but also provides satis-factory dimensions for the cross-bracing members, considering the 31-ft depth of the girder. The distance between vertical posts is 16 ft 8 in., each one coinciding with a transverse truss. This makes a convenient distance, moreover, for the lightest possible longitudinal stringers to span under the loading of the roof sheeting.

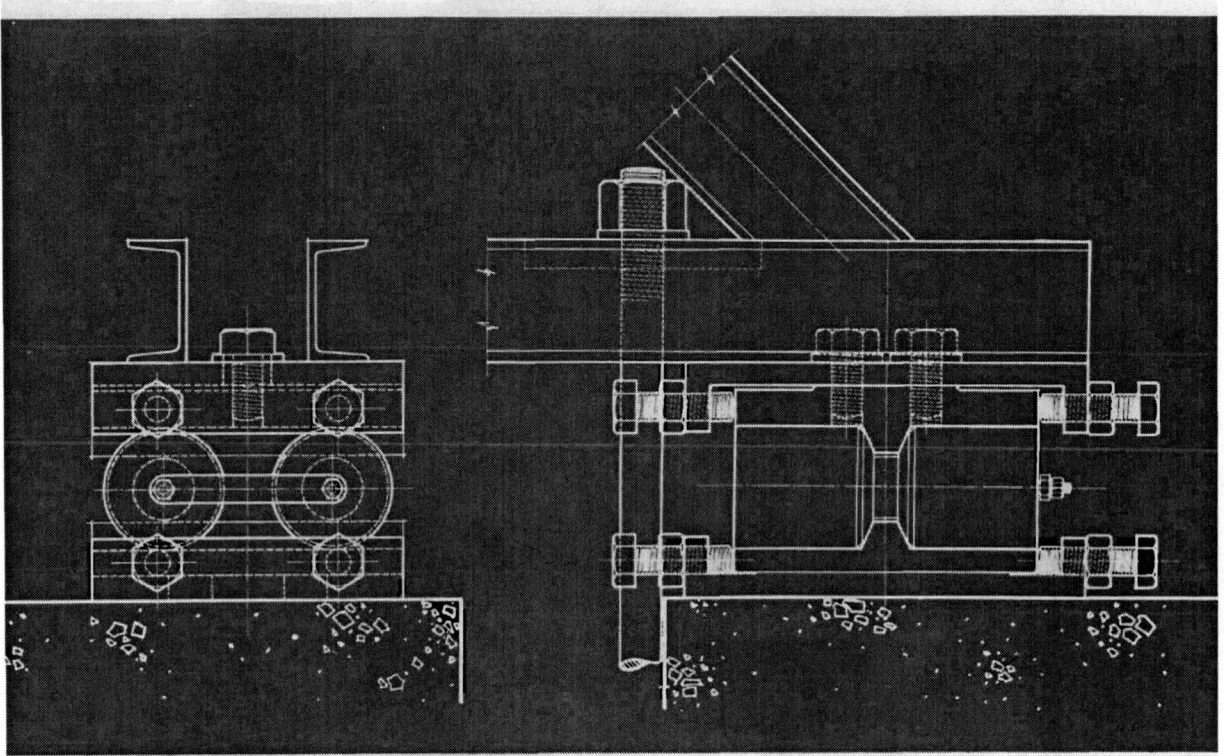

UNIDIRECTIONAL EXPANSION BEARING OF TRUSS

The horizontal component of the wind forces could have been resisted in two ways, either by a longitudinal girder transmitting horizontal shears to the lateral walls or else (and this was the solution chosen) by the transverse trussed girders carrying these forces to the rear wall. To withstand these thrusts, the rear wall was strengthened with a number of reinforced concrete batter posts.

Each transverse truss transmits the thrusts to the rear wall through grooved rollers. This arrangement allows for the longitudinal expansion of the metal structure with respect to the wall. The whole of the metal roof assembly is fixed to the midpoint of the rear wall and can freely expand on either side of it. The three vertical posts on which the main longitudinal girder is supported must allow for the free expansion of the roof structure in the directions radiating from the fixed attachment. Although these posts are rigidly embedded in the ground they are sufficiently flexible not to suffer undue bending stresses caused by

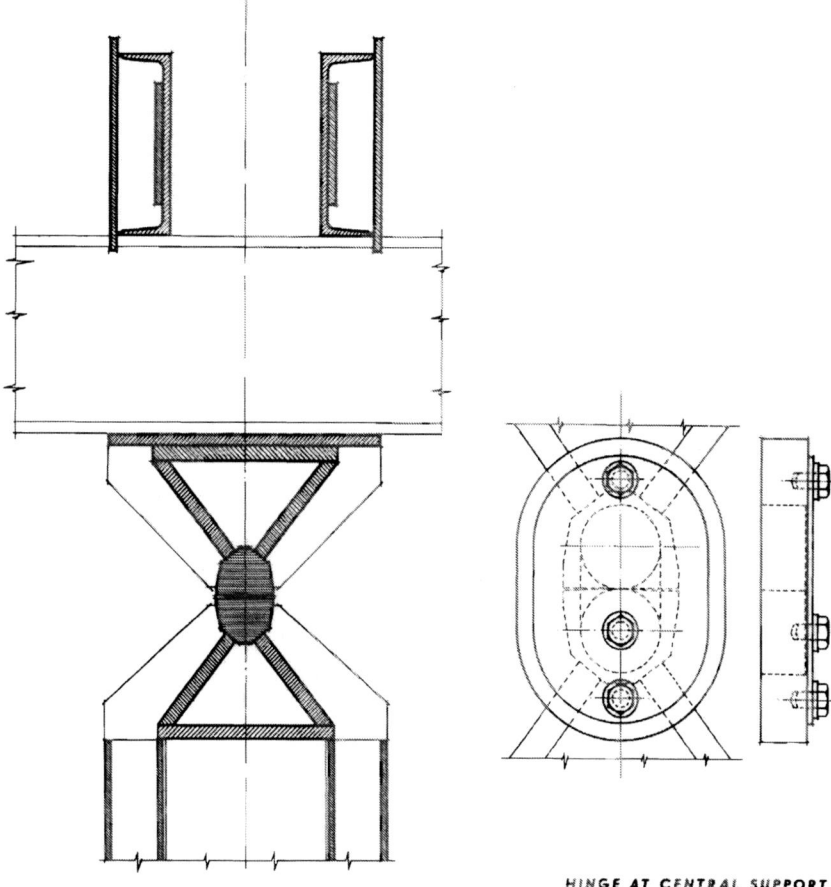

HINGE AT CENTRAL SUPPORT

the thermal expansion of the main girder, which rests upon them on flexible bearings.

The wind thrust in the longitudinal direction is not large, but nonetheless it tends to make the roof rotate about the fixed attachment at the midpoint of the rear wall. This tendency is easily restrained by the light bracing between the bottom chords of the transverse trussed girders and the capacity of the grooved bearings (through which they bear on the rear wall) to transmit horizontal forces.

To counteract any possible upward suction force of the wind, the main girder is anchored to the vertical posts by suitable links; and light, flexible connecting rods attach the trussed girder rollers to the rear wall.

An interesting feature of these hangar projects is the system of construction employed. Both roof structures were assembled in entirety on the ground and then elevated by means of hydraulic jacks to their

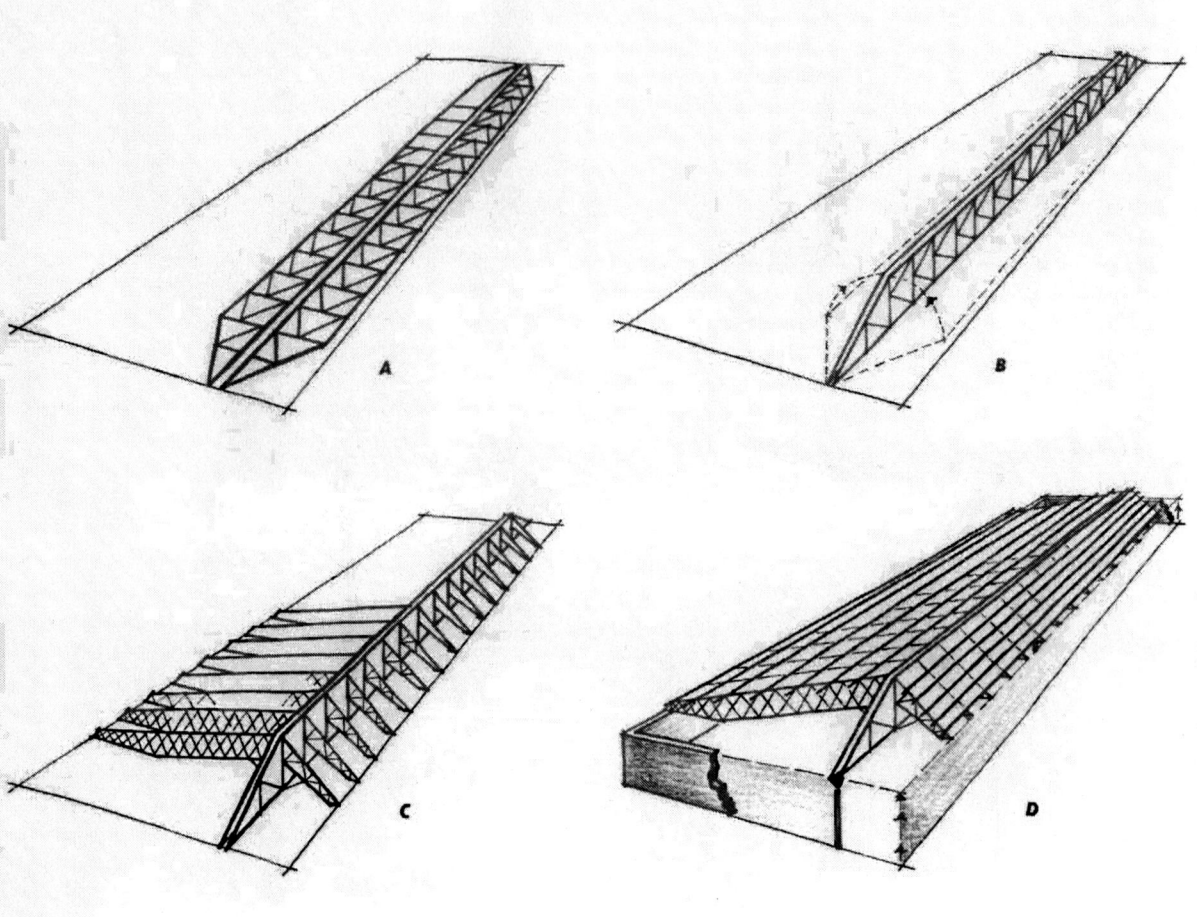

permanent position. This method avoided the need for scaffolding and workers' having to maneuver high above the ground.

As the entire structure was to be welded, for the sake of economy, it had to be designed so that this fabrication could be accomplished easily. In other words, the welding lines had to be so situated that they would be accessible when the girders were lying flat, or nearly flat, on the ground without the aid of the large rotating drums normally used to incline the part to be welded.

With this purpose in view, the main girder was made in twin halves to be joined together by gusset plates (see Fig. A). Each twin half was assembled and welded while lying flat on the ground. Then each half was turned through a right angle (Fig. B) about its lower chord, so that both halves were placed face to face in a vertical plane. In this position the final attachments and the gusset plates were welded.

The trussed girders and cantilevered trusses were fabricated in the workshop and were then welded to the vertical posts of the longitudinal girder at the building site. After the bracing members and stringers had been added, the whole roof structure was ready for lifting (Fig. C).

This final operation was accomplished by means of three hydraulic jacks placed under the three points of support of the main girder and a number of small mechanical jacks hanging from beams cantilevered from the real wall. When the roof had been lifted (Fig. D), the three posts were placed in position and the jacks were removed.

Torrejon Hangar   133

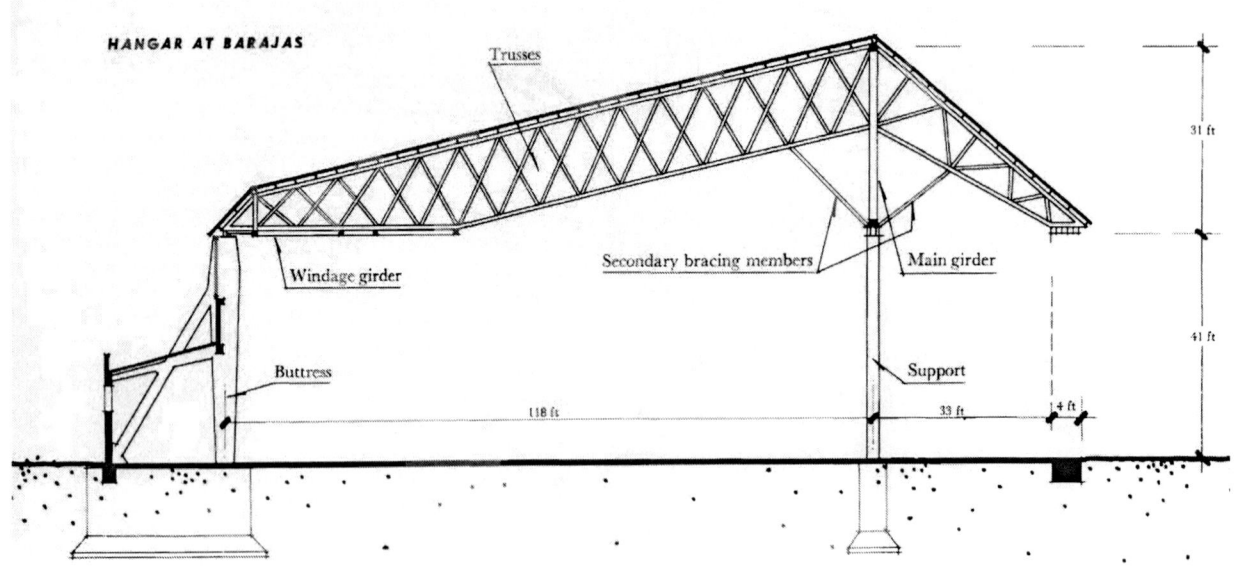

HANGAR AT BARAJAS

Trusses

Windage girder

Secondary bracing members

Main girder

Buttress

Support

31 ft

41 ft

118 ft

33 ft

4 ft

134   *Steel and Composite Structures*

The hangar at Barajas, illustrated on these two pages, is similar in size and general design to the one at Torrejon. The only difference is the greater clear height inside (41 ft) and the addition of a horizontally placed girder near the rear wall to transmit horizontal wind thrust to two heavily reinforced concrete buttresses. This arrangement avoids imposing horizontal loads on the rear wall, which projects over neighboring buildings.

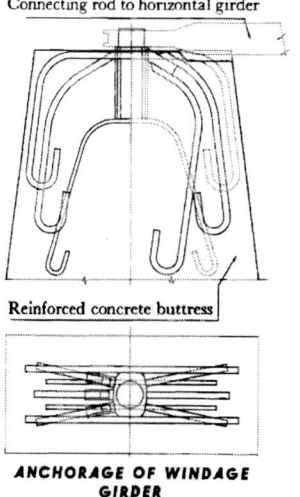

Connecting rod to horizontal girder

Reinforced concrete buttress

ANCHORAGE OF WINDAGE GIRDER

TRIANGULATED SHELL ROOFS
1948

In the Costillares Building (see page 103) and close to the dodeca-hedron, there is a long nave. It is 45 ft wide, 236 ft long, and 22 ft high. Its functional purpose demanded that it be well illuminated from the north but without direct sunlight. It is roofed by nine cylindrical vaults, each forming a 90-deg circular arc; that is, the arcs meet each other at right angles (see Fig. A, following page).

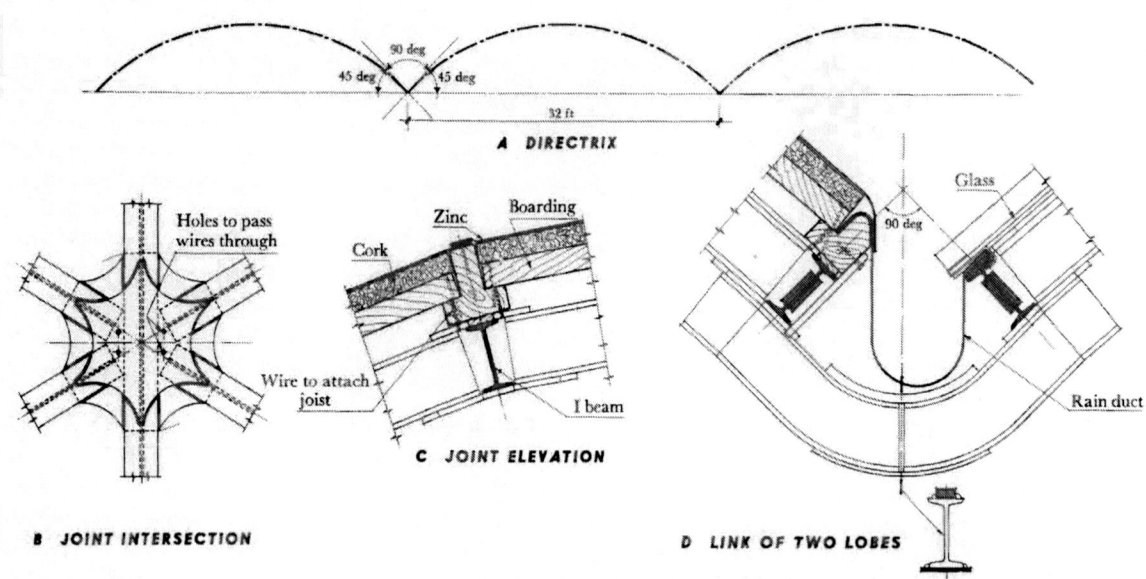

A DIRECTRIX

Holes to pass
wires through

Wire to attach
joist

B JOINT INTERSECTION

Cork   Zinc   Boarding

I beam

C JOINT ELEVATION

Glass

Rain duct

D LINK OF TWO LOBES

This type of roofing has often been constructed in continuous reinforced concrete shells. But for this project, it was found cheaper to replace the reinforced concrete with a very light, triangulated, trellised structure conforming to the cylindrical surface of the roof. It supports a continuous surface of timber planks and cork, for thermal insulation, and corrugated zinc sheeting as final cover (Fig. C).

This structure tends to behave like a continuous lamina, and its stress analysis can be performed accordingly, although of course the coefficients corresponding to thickness, rigidity, and similar properties have to be suitably chosen. All triangles are equilateral and equal in size. Hence all structural elements are identical, namely, a single I section $3\frac{1}{4}$ in. high.

These I sections are joined by welding into a continuous triangulation. Small gusset plates, one on the outer and one on the inner surface, join the I sections together by their chords (Fig. B). The inner gusset plates are attached to the flanges of the I section along longitudinal welding lines whereas the outer gussets are welded to the top flange diagonally. Because of this system, all welding can be done with the structure in its final position, that is, without its having to be turned over, as is often necessary in such work.

In fact, all the welding can be accomplished on the ground and each vault lifted as a unit to its permanent location. If this method is employed, the welding of one vault section to the next is the only job remaining at roof level.

138   *Steel and Composite Structures*

Fitting skylights into this roof presented no difficulty. It was merely a matter of affixing to the triangulated structure the small frames to support the glazing.

Rainwater is drained away by rainpipes suspended from the lower edges of the vaults (Fig. D).

A requirement of the Costillares Building was that direct sunlight be kept from entering the interior, even in summer. This end was achieved by the use of inclined screens of asbestos cement sheeting. Viewed from the side, these sunlight screens add a pleasant architectural note in the contrast of their slender flatness with the undulating roundness of the roof.

The same type of roofing could be usefully applied to large industrial buildings consisting of a series of naves, such as the one shown below, a **design** that was never constructed.

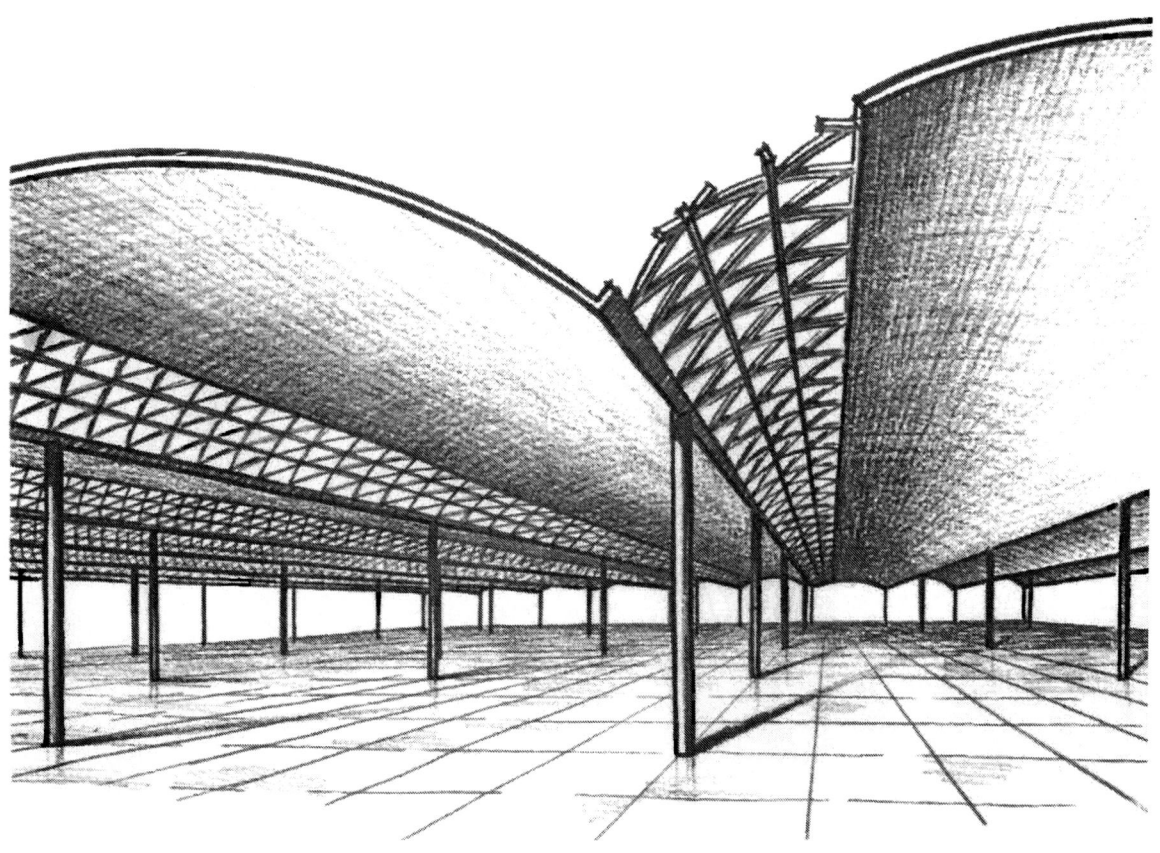

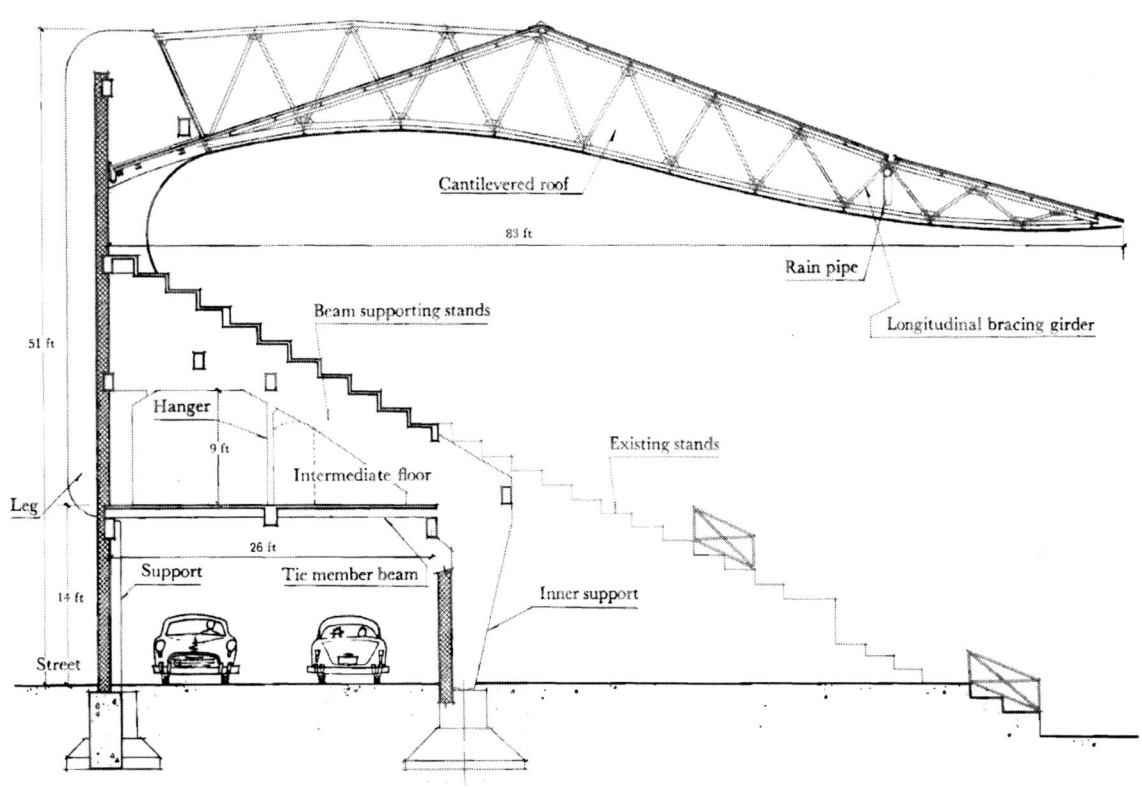

Cantilevered roof

83 ft

Rain pipe

Beam supporting stands

51 ft

Longitudinal bracing girder

Hanger

9 ft

Existing stands

Intermediate floor

Leg

26 ft

Support

Tie member beam

Inner support

14 ft

Street

LAS CORTS FOOTBALL STADIUM
1943

It was difficult to find alternatives for the structural materials and methods to be used in this great cantilevered roof. Calling for an over-hang of 8⅗ ft over the spectator stands, it had to be made in metal in order to reduce weight and cost. It had to be anchored rigidly into a vertical structure strong in bending. This structure could be made of reinforced concrete, as the heavier weight of concrete would not add to the bending moments and the cost would be cheaper.

These vertical concrete members had to have considerable depth as beams, yet it was not feasible to project them all the way to the ground with the same cross section because too much space would be pre-empted from the street or from the indoor car passage.

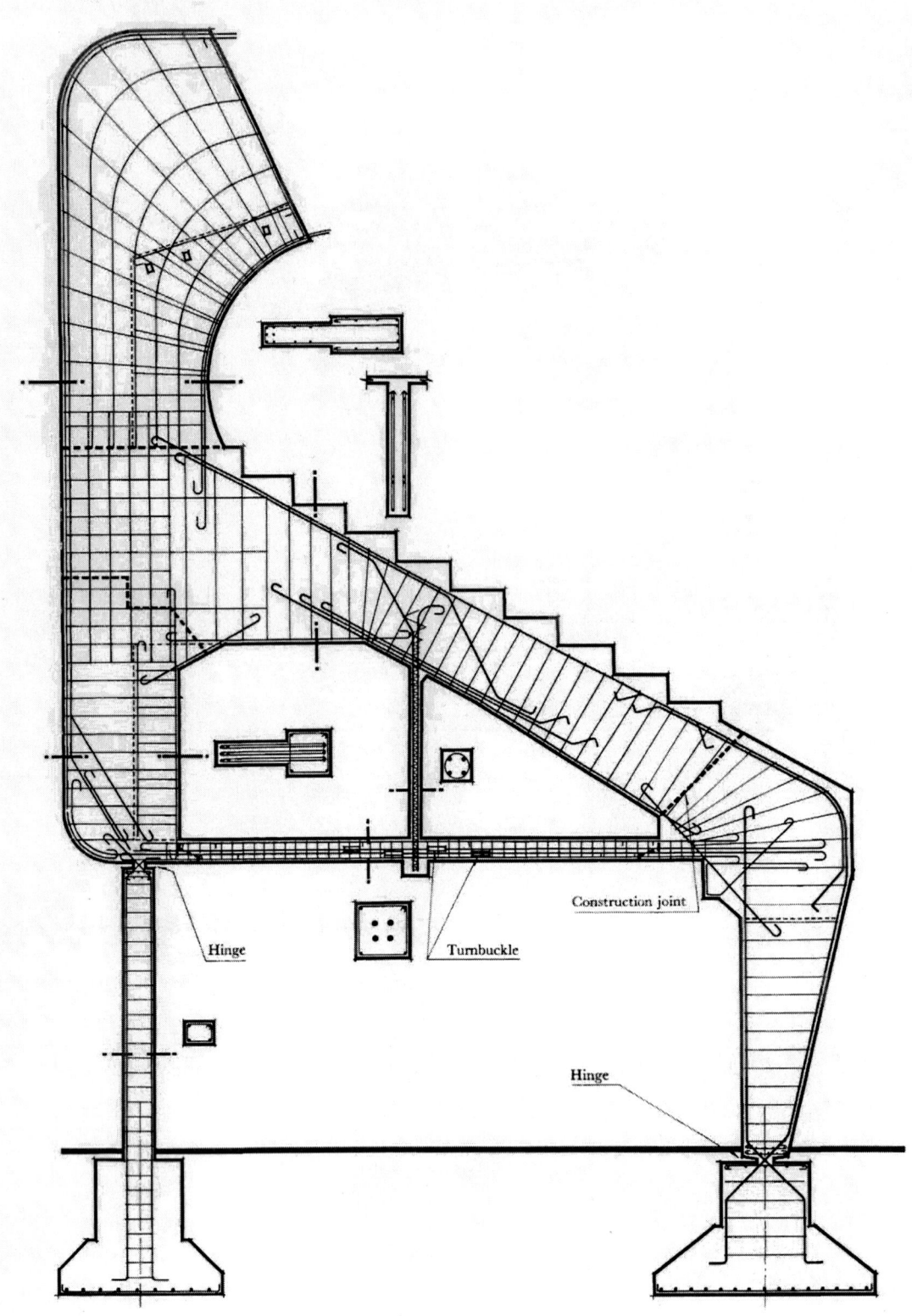

Hinge

Turnbuckle

Construction joint

Hinge

It was also unsatisfactory to transmit the full moment from the cantilevered roof along the inclined beams that support the stands, partly
because a greater beam length would be necessary and also because the
larger cross section required would limit the available height of the
galleries below the stands.

To increase the height of these galleries, it was decided to make the
horizontal tie members (also to serve as intermediate flooring for the
gallery) as thin as possible. Hence the 26-ft free span of this deck and
tie member was divided in two by supporting it at midspan with hangers suspended from the main inclined beam. Thus the flooring deck
height and its cost were decreased, and the increase in bending moment
imposed on the inclined beam supporting the stands was kept relatively

trivial, primarily because this beam forms part of a very rigid portal frame.

The stability of the whole structure depends mainly on the inner leg of the frame. This leg, situated half way down the stands (actually at the back of the old stands), does not interfere with the galleries or the covered car passage.

The intermediate flooring deck contains the tension members that counterbalance the tendency of the vertical beam to tilt forwards under the action of the cantilevered roof. The only difficulty was that the elastic elongation of these tie members might cause unduly high distor-

tions on the legs of the portal frame, and that this frame might fissure because of its great rigidity. A possible way of overcoming this difficulty might have been to insert a flexible joint midway along the inclined beam where it meets the vertical hanger. But this arrangement was unsatisfactory, because such a hinge would have decreased the stability of the whole structure under the action of wind or would have necessitated making the vertical legs far more rigid and strong. However, a simple solution was found by fitting the tie members with turnbuckles. By means of these, the tie members could be tightened beforehand so that on the erection of the cantilevered roof, the final elongation of the tie member would be the appropriate one, neither deforming the portal elements nor causing fissures. The tension in the tie member was controlled by measuring the natural frequency of the stretched bars.

The contour of the inner face of the overhanging roof could be freely chosen. The one actually selected, in addition to being airy and graceful, has the advantages of providing an uninterrupted view of the field of play and also accommodating the rain pipe with an adequate slope to drain almost all the roof. Rainwater is carried to the lateral extremities of the stand, where it falls vertically into drainage wells.

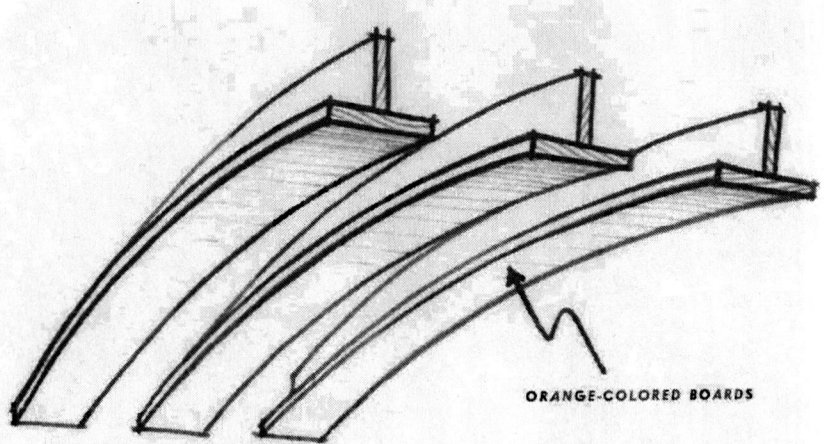

ORANGE-COLORED BOARDS

DESIGN OF UNDERSIDE OF ROOF

The roofing consists of asbestos cement sheeting. The view of the roof frame from below was dispersed with a semicontinuous surface of orange-colored timber planks with 6-in. gaps between each plank. This device emphasizes the inflexed outline of the intrados and at the same time gives the cantilevered roof a combined impression of plastic strength and lightness.

The transverse cantilevered girders are spaced every 17 ft. Each of them is anchored to the reinforced concrete structure by means of bolts that attach the top chord of the overhanging girder directly to the steel reinforcement of the concrete. To ensure an even deflection of the free edge, the transverse cantilevers are connected by a light longitudinal bracing girder running at a distance of 17 ft from the roof boundary.

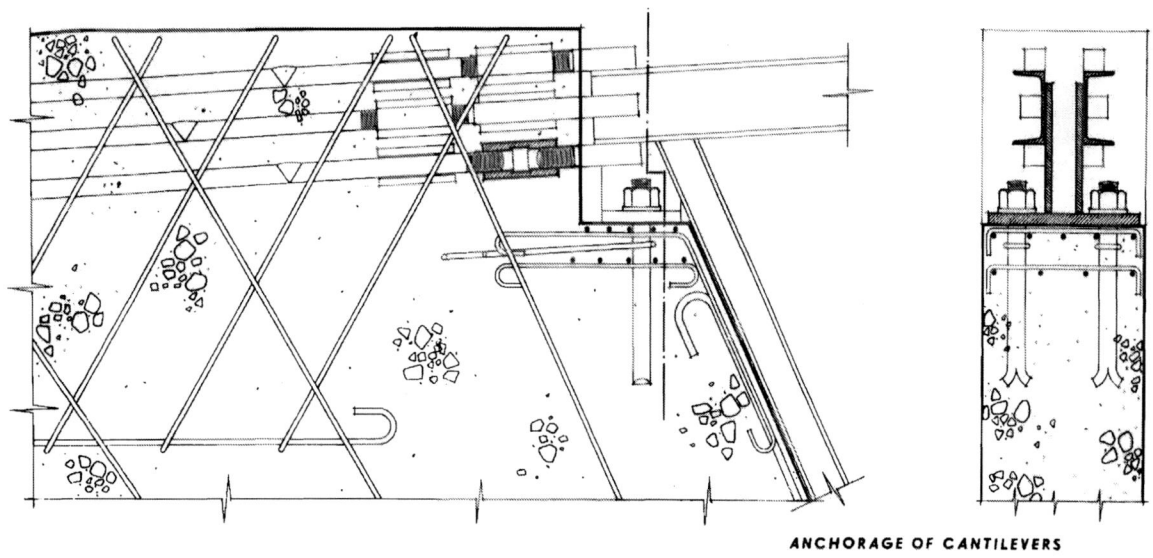

ANCHORAGE OF CANTILEVERS

TORDERA BRIDGE

COMPOSITE STEEL AND REINFORCED
CONCRETE BRIDGES
1939

It has always been taken for granted that the concrete in reinforced concrete structures is meant to take the compressive loads, whereas the steel is provided mainly to resist the tensile forces. This principle leads logically to the design of triangulated structures in which the parts working mainly in tension are made of steel, whereas those in which the main loads are compressive are made of lightly reinforced concrete.

In general, concrete serves as a cheaper means of withstanding compressive loads than steel, but it is practically incapable of resisting tensile forces. Steel is well suited to the latter purpose. For light, slender members, it can also act in compression, but less well, because the danger of buckling intrinsic in slenderness limits the working stress of steel far more than it is limited in tension. Consequently, if the ratio of tensile to compressive loads is of the right order, a metal member is the best solution.

In many situations, reinforced concrete not only does not save steel, but by being heavier and causing the total dead weight to increase, may even involve the use of a larger over-all amount of steel. In members subject only to tension, concrete is useful only as a means of preventing the corrosion of the steel. But a good paint serves this purpose nearly as well and without overloading the structure.

Conversely, even though it may need light reinforcement to give it cohesion and strength to withstand parasitic stresses due to shrinkage and other causes, concrete is the appropriate material for members working mainly in compression. It becomes even more desirable when it can fulfill other functional requirements as well. A case in point is a bridge deck, which requires continuous slabs for support of the actual pavement surface.

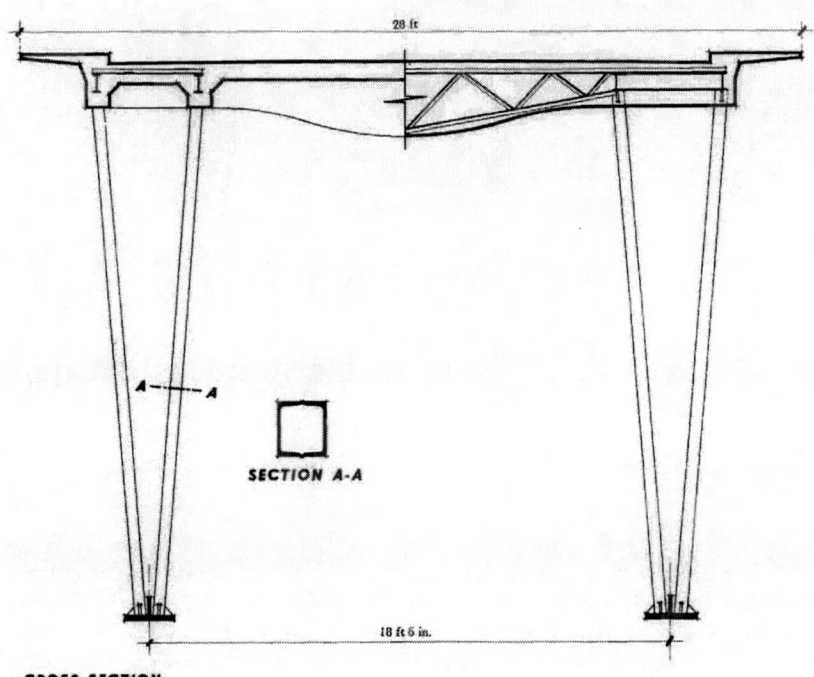

28 ft

A---A

SECTION A-A

18 ft 6 in.

CROSS SECTION

It is only logical to make such slabs function as the compression elements of the bridge girders (thus predetermining to a certain extent the bridge design). In such an arrangement, it is preferable for the bridge girder to run below the deck level.

The application of these general principles to the Tordera Bridge led to the design shown on the following pages. The project marked the first time I had employed a composite construction of metal and reinforced concrete for a relatively large span.

The tension beam follows an elliptical arc. This design was chosen after trying several other methods for achieving a fairly constant load along the whole length of the chord while keeping the compressive stresses in the diagonals low enough to avoid buckling. The most heavily loaded diagonals are the end ones, which are also the shortest. Their box section is adequately stable.

To reduce secondary stresses as much as possible, the tension chord (shown below) consists of horizontal metal strips with only a slight vertical flange. This flange is just sufficiently stiff to resist the bending moment caused by the weight of the unsupported length of the strip itself, as moments at the joints of the lower chord and the diagonals are negligible. The same desire to reduce secondary forces led to the omission of transverse bracings between the elliptical beams. Each cross section of the bridge as shown on the opposite page consists of two V-shaped members. These start from two separate points on the transverse deck joints and converge to a panel point on the elliptical beam. In addition to providing lateral stability for the tension chord, these V-shaped members also support the transverse deck joists as simply supported beams.

The development of such composite structures did not progress until arc welding techniques had made it possible to fabricate joints of sufficient compactness to be embedded in concrete without endangering it. The classical joints using riveted gusset plates tended to produce shearing effects along these knifelike plates that were too hazardous for the concrete. And the bonding between both materials often failed because of the tendency of concrete to shrink.

DETAIL OF LOWER JOINT

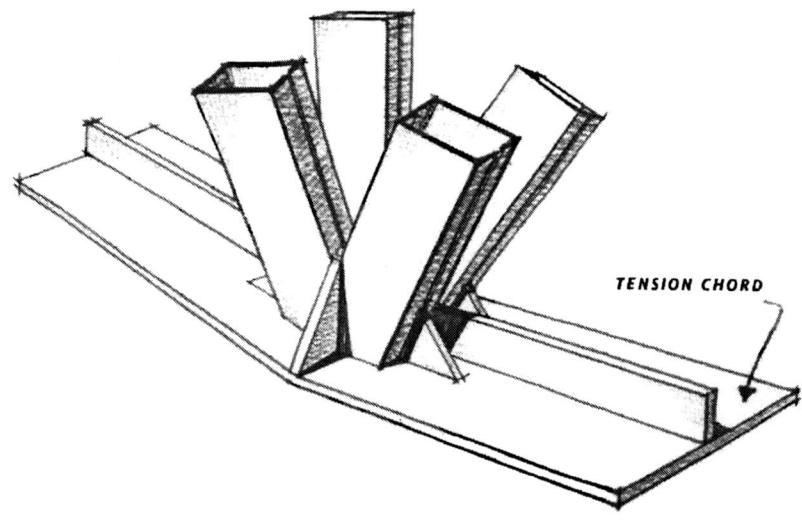

TENSION CHORD

Tordera Bridge   153

Nowadays these defects are easily overcome, thanks to the freedom enjoyed by the engineer in designing suitably compact welded joints.

As concrete is not so strong a material as steel, joints have to be made in a special way so that the loads from the steel can be distributed over a sufficiently wide surface of the concrete.

This purpose is well served by embedding large transverse bearing plates in the concrete, or by welding a number of anchorage rods to the metal member and hooking them at the ends. The concrete can be further reinforced against local compressive stresses by holding it together with hoops or grids. But a discussion of these various devices belongs more to a textbook than to this volume.

When the secondary stresses of the Tordera Bridge were calculated, account was taken of varying deformation in the different materials. For concrete, the modulus of deformation (that is, the stress-strain ratio

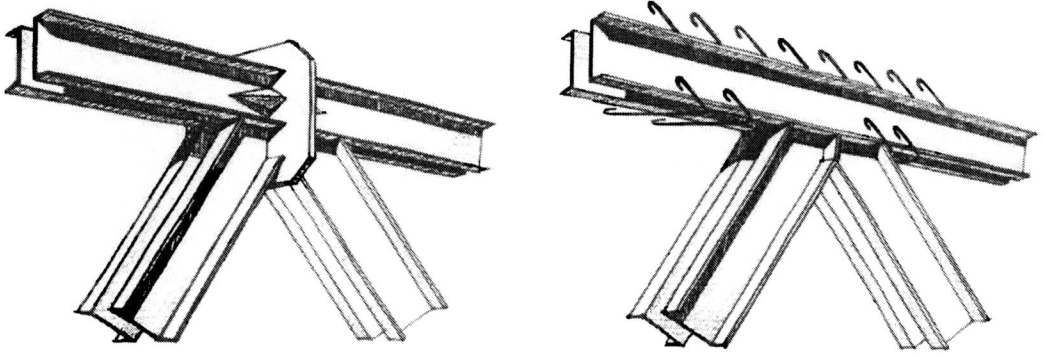

PLATE WELDED TO TOP CHORD   BARS WELDED TO TOP CHORD

in a not perfectly elastic material) was assumed to be half that indicated by normal tests in order to allow for the plastic deformation of the concrete during the first months, and even years, of its permanently compressed state. Later it was found that the deck had shrunk by less than 2 in.

Allowance was also made for the possible difference in temperature of the exposed steel and concrete parts. Later observations and checks on the bridge confirmed the design assumptions. The trial overloads were applied slowly from 8 A.M. till 2 P.M.; simultaneously, the deforma-

Tordera Bridge   155

tions of every part of the bridge were recorded. During this phase of
the test, the bridge deflected upwards instead of downwards. The ex-
planation is quite simple. Early in the morning the sun heated the
lower chord, causing it to expand. But as the sun rose into the sky, the
lower chords became protected by the shade of the deck, whereas the

deck itself, which was the compression beam, got warmed up. Thus the top chord expanded at the same time as the lower one cooled down and contracted. And the upward deflection caused by this phenomenon was greater than the opposite effects caused by the applied overload.

The old Tordera Bridge—near Barcelona —had been blown up during the Spanish War. The piers remained, but it was necessary to provide new spans. These included two 150-ft approaches and a central span of 180 ft. To keep the lowest part of the girders at the same level in the three spans, the longitudinal outline of the deck was made

parabolic, that is, higher at the center of the bridge than at the approaches. The slight curvature of the deck also improves its appearance, although this aspect was not especially important considering that the bridge may be viewed from the side only by leaving the road and making a special trip down to the river bank.

The girders are provided with a light metal compression chord designed to carry only the weight of the steel structure itself and a single longitudinal layer of concrete. With the addition of this concrete

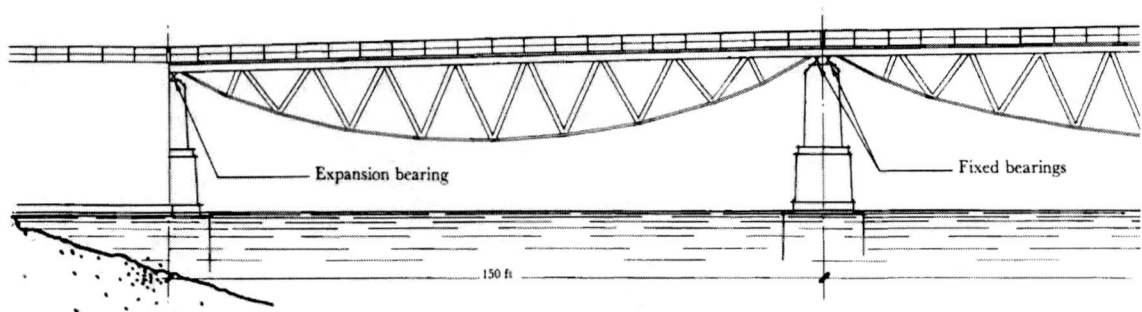

Expansion bearing   Fixed bearings

150 ft

LA MUGA BRIDGE

layer to the compression chord, the girders become sufficiently strong to carry the weight of the whole concrete deck. And in turn, the addition of the deck makes the whole structure capable of supporting the rolling overloads for which it was designed.

The steel girders were erected by running them longitudinally into position (see page 155) even though the curved shape of their lower chords did not make them ideally suited for this operation. This shape, as explained previously, was chosen simply for mechanical reasons.

The same type of bridge can also be constructed with girders of constant depth, for example, the bridge over the Muga river seen above. This project called for three girders to be run longitudinally into position, one behind the other, and then welded together so as to behave

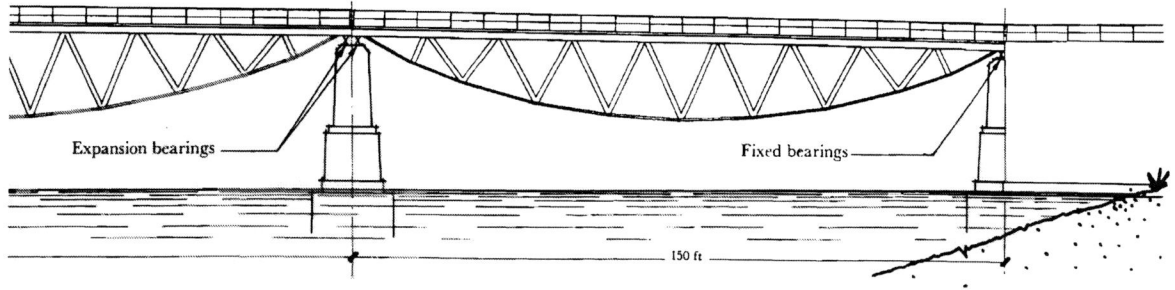

Expansion bearings

Fixed bearings

150 ft

La Muga Bridge   159

as a continuous beam of three spans (operation shown above). Once in final position, each span was cut from the next by blowtorch, thereby becoming simply supported and independent; and finally the traffic decks, which serve functionally as the compression chord, were concreted.

Experience has indicated that this type of design can be constructed with a beam running continuously over several piers, and if I had to design another such bridge, I would adopt this method. I should merely reinforce with concrete the bottom metal chord in the region of the piers where it is in compression.

The weight of this additional concrete would add only slightly to the over-all magnitude of the bending moments.

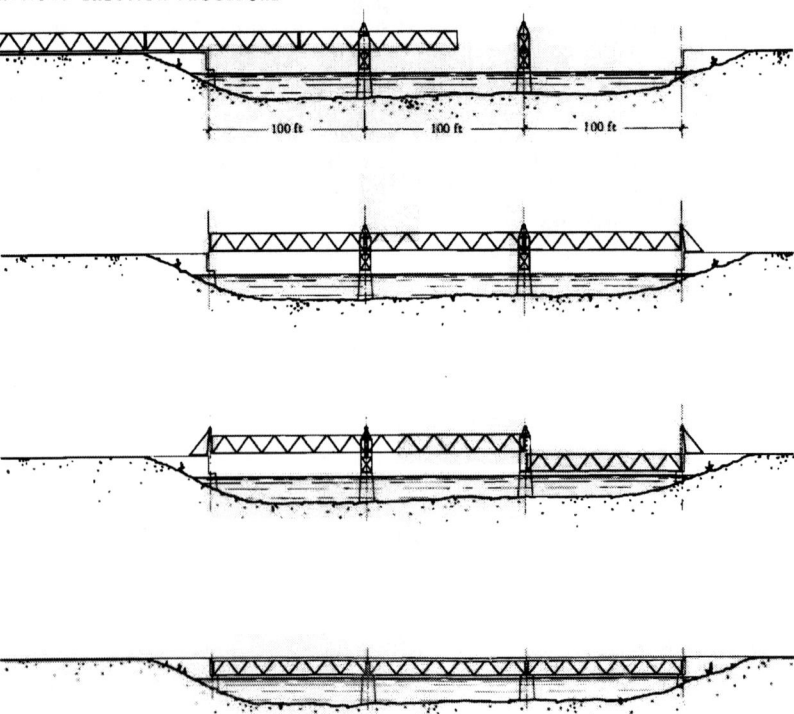

LA MUGA ERECTION PROCEDURE

The saving in cost resulting from this composite type of construction may be very considerable. Each case is different, of course, but for the Tordera Bridge it was estimated that the adopted design meant a saving of 25 per cent over conventional practice, despite the fact this was my first project of the type. At the time, I did not dare specify a continuous girder of composite steel and concrete construction. However, the satisfactory behavior of such structures since 1947 now justifies their construction with even longer spans.

5 CHURCHES AND CHAPELS

VILLAVERDE CHURCH

PONT DE SUERT CHURCH

SANCTI SPIRIT

CHAPEL OF THE ASCENSION, XERRALLO

SKETCHES FOR OTHER CHAPELS

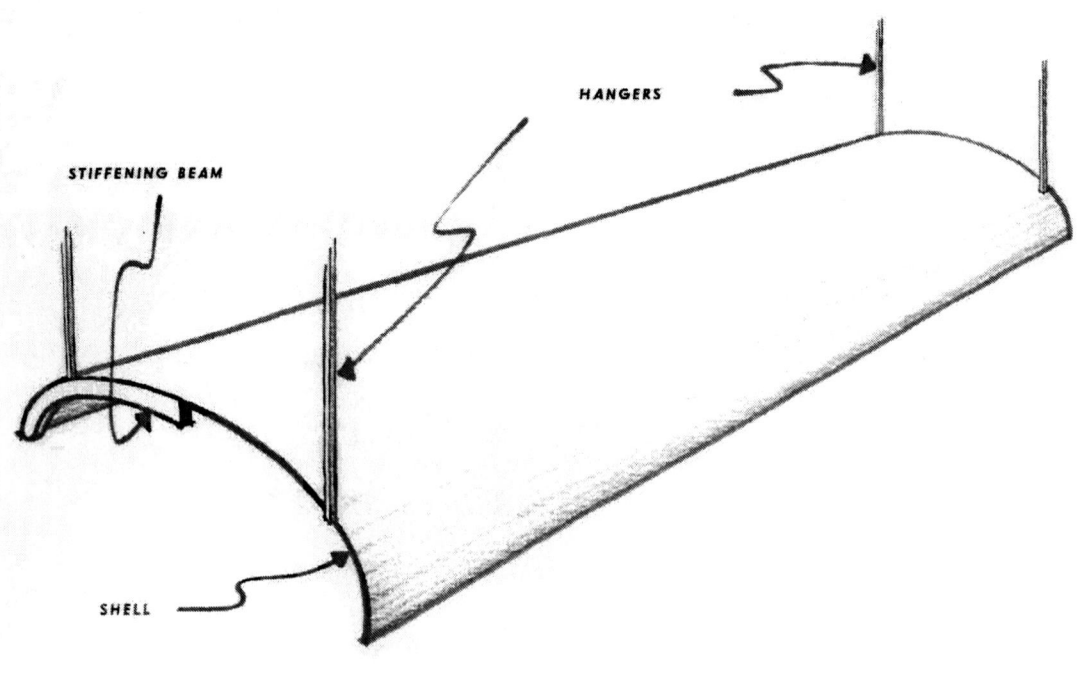

GYMNASIUM COURTYARD ROOF

HANGERS

STIFFENING BEAM

SHELL

164

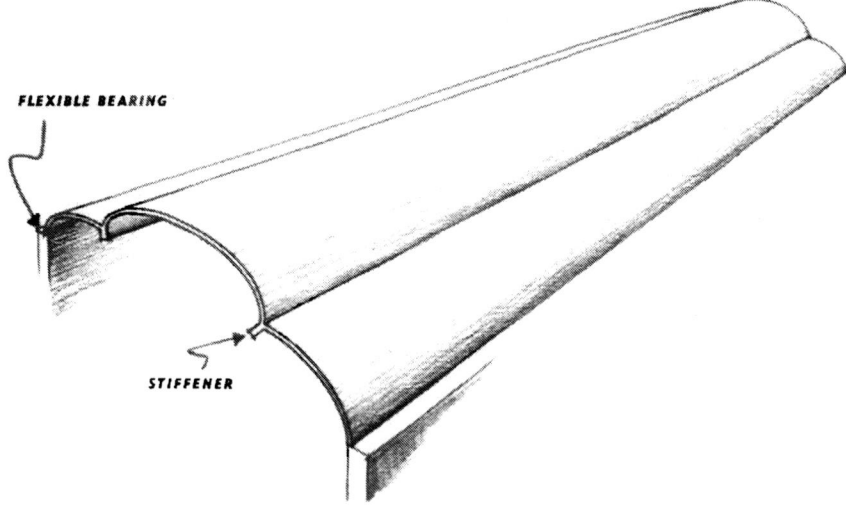

FLEXIBLE BEARING

STIFFENER

VAULT AT VILLAVERDE

VILLAVERDE CHURCH
1935

The first thin shell of reinforced concrete that the author had occasion to build was the roof for a gymnasium courtyard (opposite page). It had a 72-ft span and was 26 ft wide. It was a cylindrical shell, of semi-elliptical outline, 2 in. thick. As the first solid ground was 20 ft below the surface, it was thought more economical to do without the usual supports and foundations and hang the whole laminar roof from four points anchored on the walls of existing buildings.

A somewhat more important project is the roof of the church at Villaverde (above). This also consists of a shell vault of cylindrical

165

shape, but the directrix is formed by a semiellipse in the center and a
quarter ellipse on each side. The vault is supported in entirety at its
two ends, one of which allows for the free longitudinal expansion of
the lamina.

The main tensile forces are concentrated at the intersecting edges, along which the lateral lobes meet the central one. A rib runs along these edges that contains the longitudinal reinforcement necessary to withstand the tensile forces.

Besides the surface stresses induced in such structures by the behavior of the lamina as a beam, account must also be taken of the transverse bending. The latter, although relatively small, is certainly not negligible in relation to the thickness of the shell. It is usually calculated by means of the simplified hypotheses and methods of Finsterwalder, which are now accepted as standard practice for this purpose.

The church dome consists of an octagonal shell, also 2 in. thick and supported wholly on two diametrically opposed sides of the octagon.

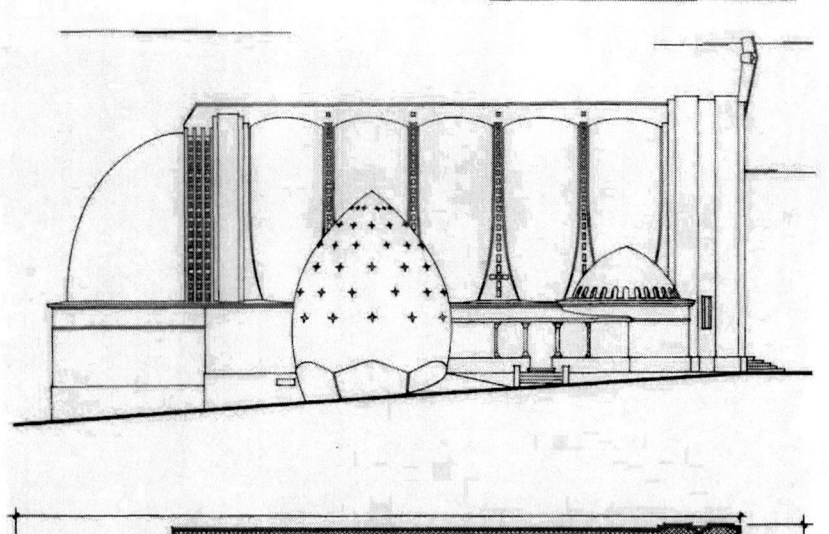

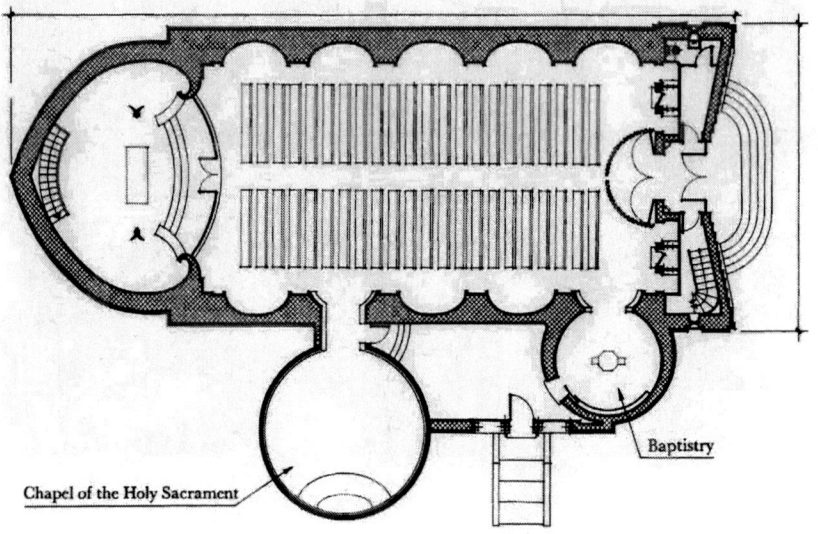

Chapel of the Holy Sacrament

Baptistry

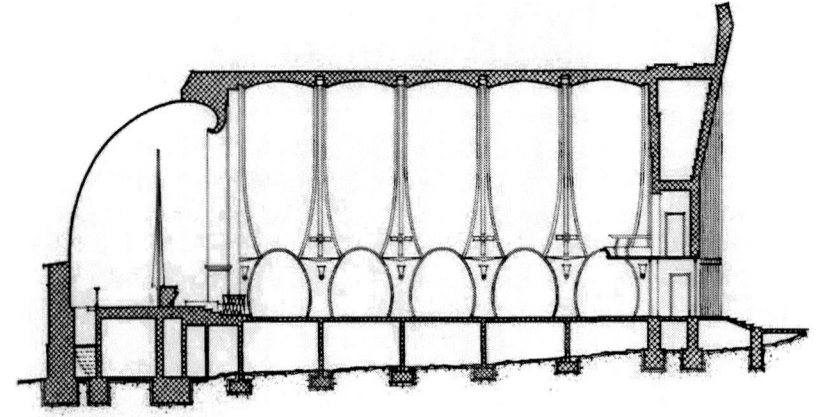

168

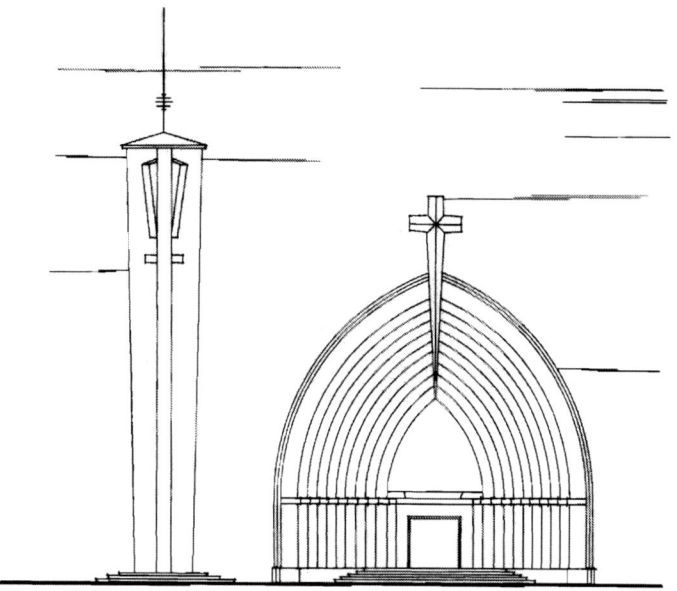

PONT DE SUERT CHURCH
1952

Hidden among the lofty crags of the Pyrenees, the Ribagorzana valley still contains architectural relics of primitive pre-Romanesque art. In this valley, the village of Pont de Suert has experienced an unexpected increase in the limited variety of its buildings with the construction of a new community development by the Empresa Nacional Hidroeléctrica del Ribagorzana for their personnel.

This corporation also decided to build a church that would be modern and constructed in accordance with present-day construction techniques, yet not mark a break with time-honored Catholic tradition and liturgy. It was not to upset the religious customs of the district nor the residents' idea of what a church should be by introducing too radical architectural innovations.

The nave of the church is straightforward. It is comprised of equilateral ogival vaults. The cross on the facade projects dynamically forward, beyond the building proper. The belfry rises by itself, separate from the church building. It consists of three ribs converging at angles of 120 deg. The apse is of classical design. The circular baptistry is

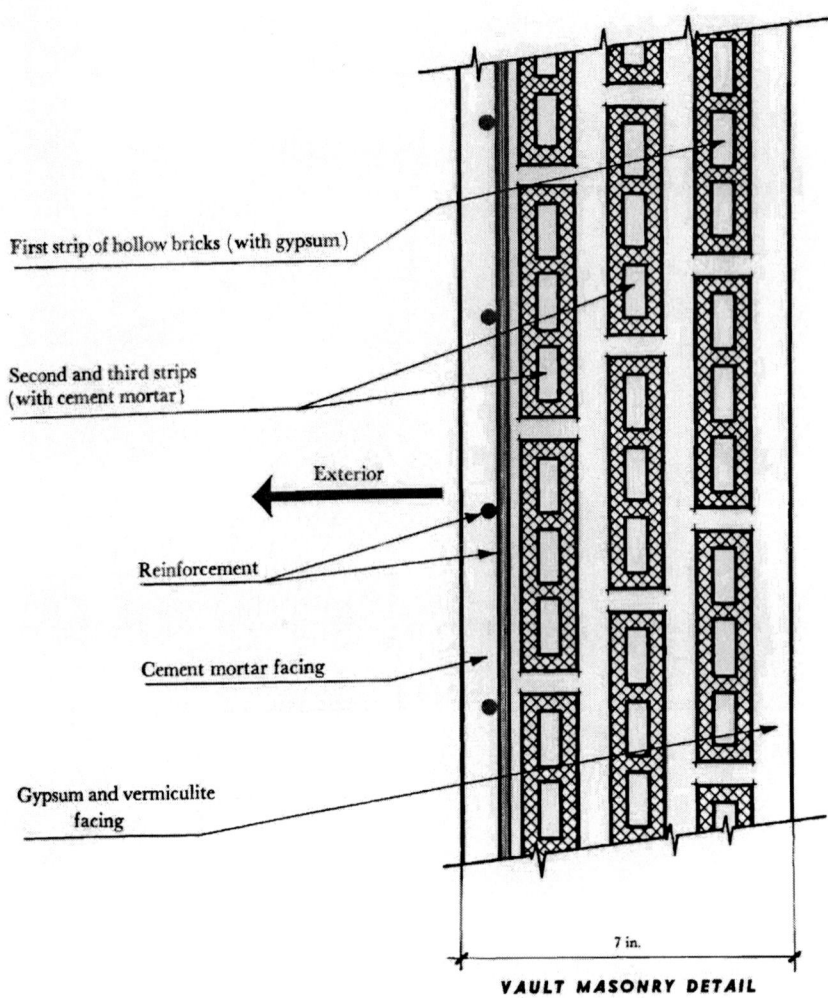

First strip of hollow bricks (with gypsum)

Second and third strips
(with cement mortar)

Exterior

Reinforcement

Cement mortar facing

Gypsum and vermiculite
facing

7 in.

VAULT MASONRY DETAIL

placed on the left of the nave at the main entry. The sacristy and paro-
chial office are arranged with an independent entrance along the side
wall of the church. Finally, there is a special chapel for the Holy
Sacrament.

The vertical walls of stone masonry lack special features. But the
vaults are somewhat novel both in form and structure. They consist
of three layers of thin hollow brick 1 3/16 in. thick, placed end to end.
The first layer is joined with quick-setting cement in order to dispense
with the need of supporting formwork. The other two layers are constructed with ordinary cement mortar in which a thin wire reinforcement is embedded. The inner surface is covered with vermiculite and

gypsum to improve its sound and heat absorption properties, and the exterior is covered by a mosaic layer.

As the roof has the same shape outside as inside, the basic structure of the entire edifice is visible.

Such shells are cheap to make and may be adapted to any desired shape, even to continuously changing curvatures, as evidenced by all the roof vaults of this church. If constructed by bricklayers skilled in the technique, they can be made without the aid of formwork. The only thing necessary is a set of guides to indicate to the craftsman the contours to be followed. These guides are spaced more or less closely, depending on the degree of the curvature.

In the nave of Pont de Suert, the roof shell adopts the general curves of ogival arches, although the transverse curvature of each element is variable, being greatest at the springing and flattening out towards the apex. The shape of these lobes bears some resemblance to sea shells.

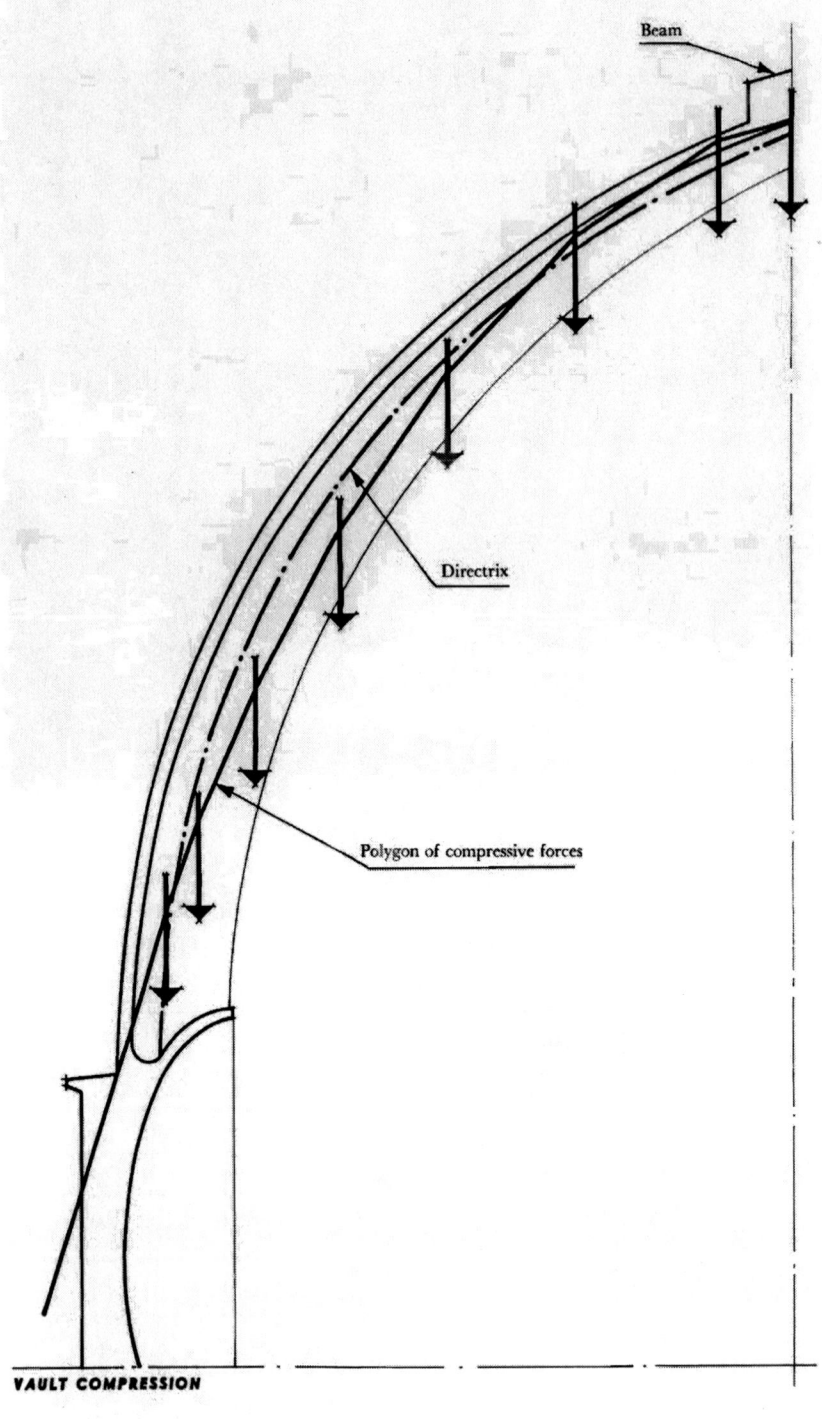

Beam

Directrix

Polygon of compressive forces

VAULT COMPRESSION

172   *Churches and Chapels*

The base of each lobe merges with an alcove, thereby imparting a sense of lightness to the lower walls. Their transverse curvature decreases towards the loftier part of the vault so that a feeling of increasing lightness is projected from the top as well. The shape of the lobes adapts itself well to the bending moments acting on it.

A longitudinal beam of reinforced concrete runs along the crown at the intersection of the vaulted lobes of the roof. This beam is visible only from the exterior. Besides stiffening the roof structure, it gives sufficient weight to the roof crown to cause the funicular of forces in the vaults to approximate the vaults' ogival contour. However, this funicular does not coincide exactly with the directrix of the arch (see diagram at left). The deviation causes local bending, and hence there are variations in the stresses between one zone of the transverse section and another, which in turn imply different radial components at different points of the section. Consequently, a transverse strip of shell is subjected to bending forces (shown below) that have to be withstood with the aid of its reinforcement in the same way as in reinforced concrete shells.

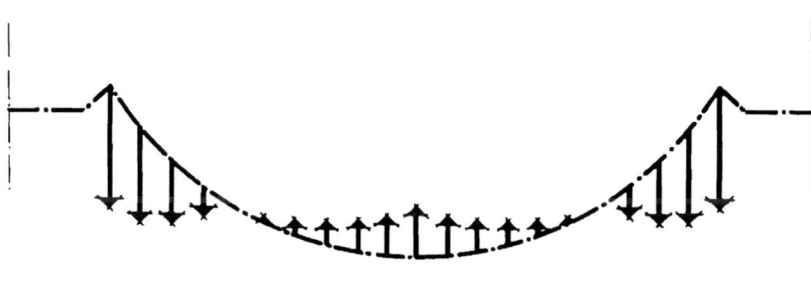

BENDING FORCES

Thermal changes, particularly differences between the inner and outer temperature of the structure, also add to these local bending moments and must be taken into account.

For this particular roof, it was thought adequate to embed a reinforcement within the outer cement facing, but it would also have been practicable to have placed additional reinforcement either between the layers of brick or within an inner cement facing.

The width of the lobes is narrower at the springing, where the curvature is greatest, than at the crown, where the curvature is least. Therefore between neighboring lobes there remain wedge-like sections of

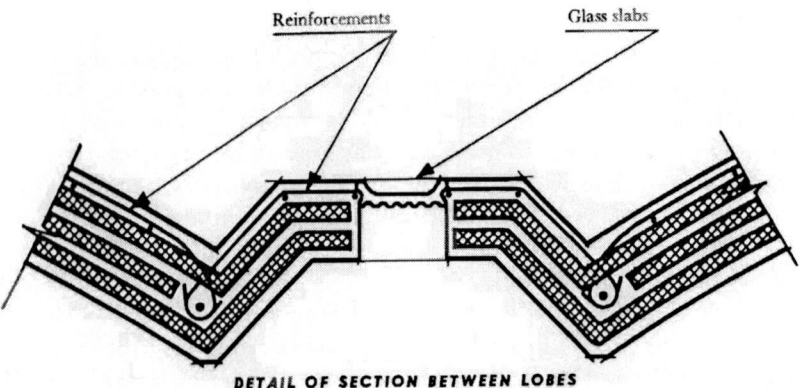

Reinforcements   Glass slabs

DETAIL OF SECTION BETWEEN LOBES

cylindrical vault; these have been fitted with pressed glass slabs (diagram above) to illuminate the nave. These segments of cylindrical surface also serve to give rigidity to the edges of the lobes, which would otherwise buckle under the local concentration of forces.

The cupola that forms the apse (below) is constructed of the same material as the lobes, and its cross-sectional shape is that of a logarithmic spiral, the pole of which lies on the contour of the opening of the nave into the apse.

STATION OF THE CROSS

Pont de Suert Church   175

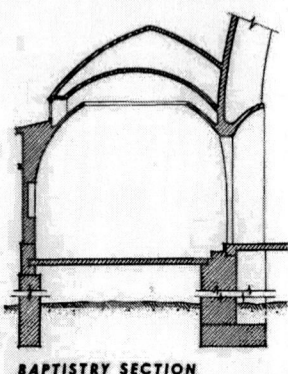

BAPTISTRY SECTION

The baptistry is covered by a double cupola (cross section at left). The outer one has windows round it, and these are screened by the inner shell, which is open at the top. Light therefore enters the inner shell by reflection from the outer one, which represents the celestial vault.

The chapel of the Holy Sacrament stands out in studied differentiation from the main building of the church. Outwardly its shape is reminiscent of a pineapple. Its surface is punctuated with small glass slabs to let in daylight. Inside, the shape is similar, but the top part is made distinctive by an inner dome suspended from the main structure.

Pobla Segur, courtesy J. L. de Turismo

The whole design aims at revealing the laminar structure fully, including the volumes that it encloses. No structural part is hidden, and those that are not structural are not visible, because there are none. All the strength is provided by the interplay of curved thin shells.

The altar is of stone, and on either side of it two palms rise to embrace the sanctuary, the design of which rhymes with that of the apse. Between the palms and supported by very thin, almost invisible wires, a slender, smooth cross is silhouetted in midair against a background of light.

SANCTI SPIRIT
1953

Far above the last hamlet of the valley at an altitude of about 5,000 ft , the waters of the San Nicolau stream, tired of cascading downwards, slow up for a while and idle and meander down gentle slopes before hurling themselves again down an even deeper gorge. For most of the year this region is snowbound, but in summer it is a delectable spot for the rambler and the trout fisherman. Only an occasional storm, sudden, violent and brief, is apt to upset the peacefulness of this paradise.

Should one occur, however, the tourist can find refuge under this hemispherical shelter, the shell of which is oriented to leeward. And he can while away the time until the shower is over by looking at the sculptured dove inspired by the name of the place, Sancti Spirit.

Situated at a river bend, the shelter rests on a platform in the shape of a boat. Its half cupola rises above like a full sail in the wind.

This half cupola made of reinforced brick masonry was constructed with the same technique used in the Pont de Suert Church. Its curvature is slightly sharpened along its line of symmetry. The free edge of the lamina needs increased rigidity; and to prevent it from bending or buckling, a number of light rods radiate from two fixed points in the foundation slab to various points of the free edge of the shell.

These tie members, which also serve as decorative pattern when viewed from the front, were post-tensioned before the centering of the

shell was removed. Equal loading was thereby assured in some such way as that obtained in the spokes of a bicycle wheel.

No practical method exists at present whereby the stress calculation of such shells can be made. But this drawback should be no reason why such shells, even ones much larger than this small shelter, should not be constructed. There are always experimental methods for investigating their strength in those laboratories and research centers specializing in modern techniques of stress analysis.

To imagine and to design such shells, however, it is necessary to possess a certain intuitive knowledge—very easy to acquire—of their stress and strength properties so that only the most appropriate shapes will be selected. Their actual suitability can then be checked by analysis or experiment.

This particular shelter could also have been made in timber, and with this in mind I sketched out the designs shown on these two pages.

Finally, however, it was decided to construct the shell first described.

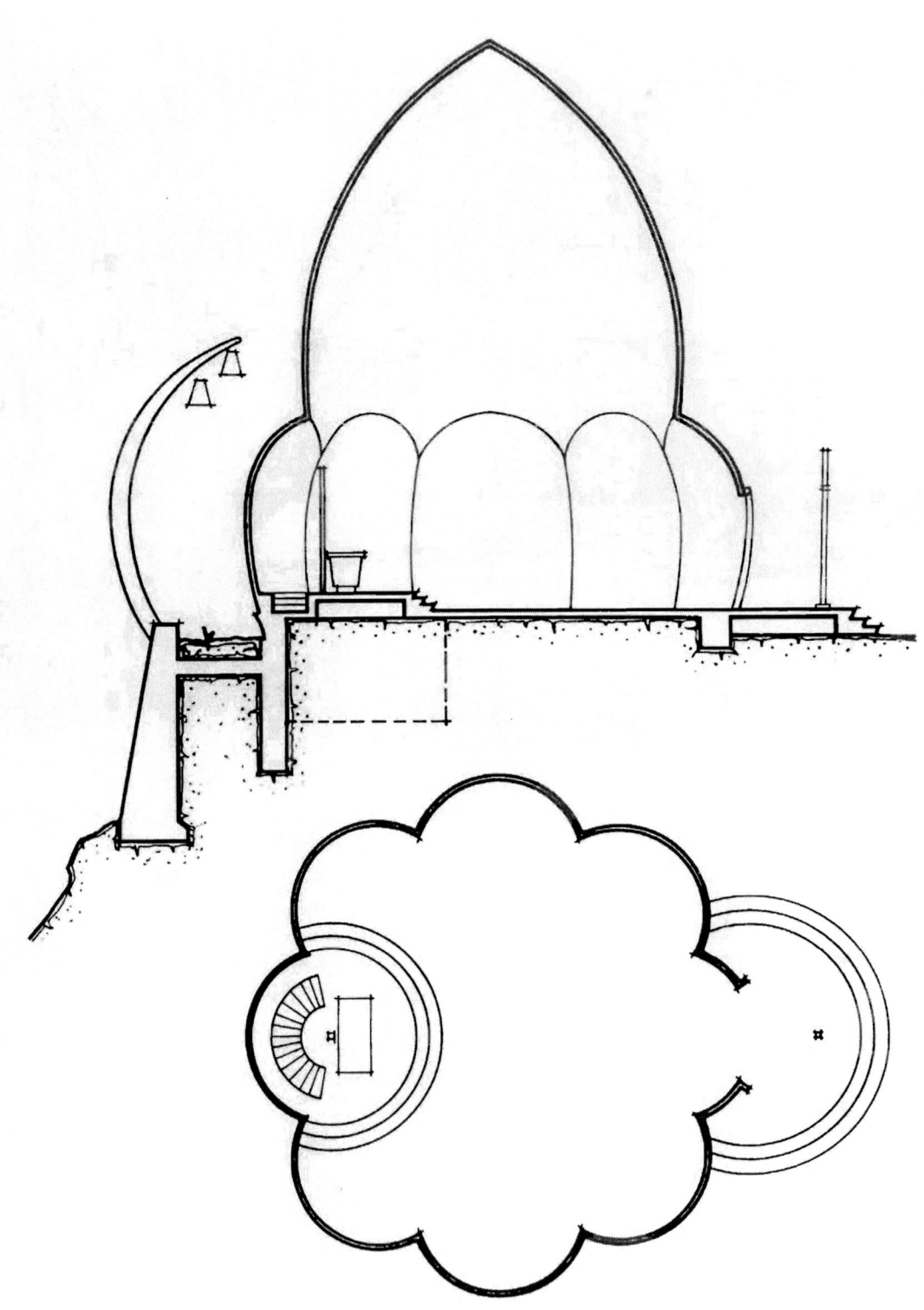

THE CHAPEL OF THE ASCENSION AT XERRALLO
1952

Near Xerrallo, a spur on a steep mountain side forms a small level area. This was the site chosen for a chapel for the small local congregation.

I imagined the humble people grouped around their God of Plenty in their tiny shelter overlooking the abyss. This symbolism led me to design a circular chapel with a considerably canted dome resting on eight small cupolas and opening inwards. It would have been easy to build it of reinforced brick in the manner of the Pont de Suert chapel. But when I went to the building site to measure out the plan, I discovered I had misjudged the available space. The circular chapel I had designed would necessarily extend beyond the horizontal platform, which was narrower than I had thought and allowed only for a triangular shaped building.

ORIGINAL DESIGN

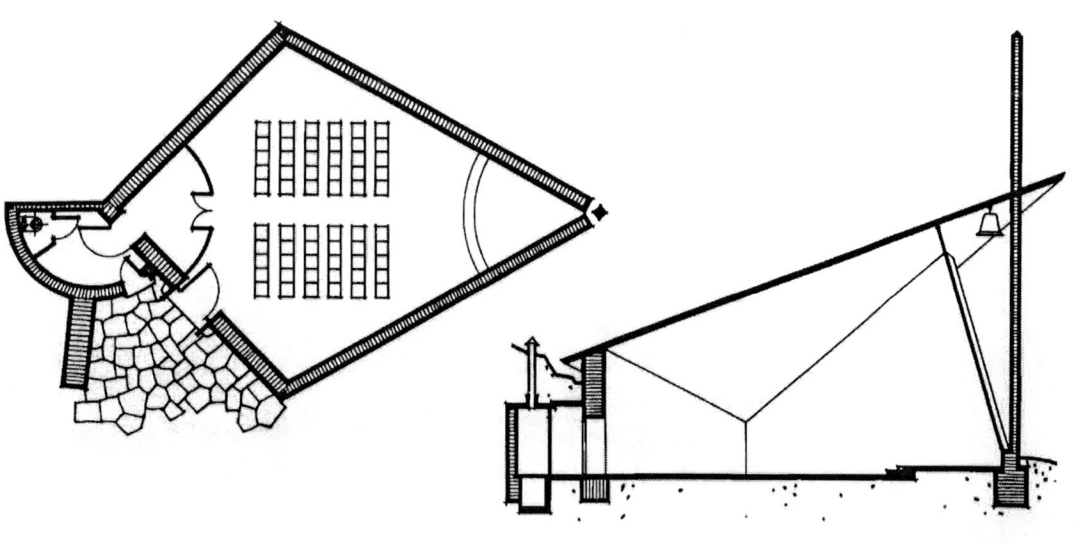

Xerrallo Chapel 189

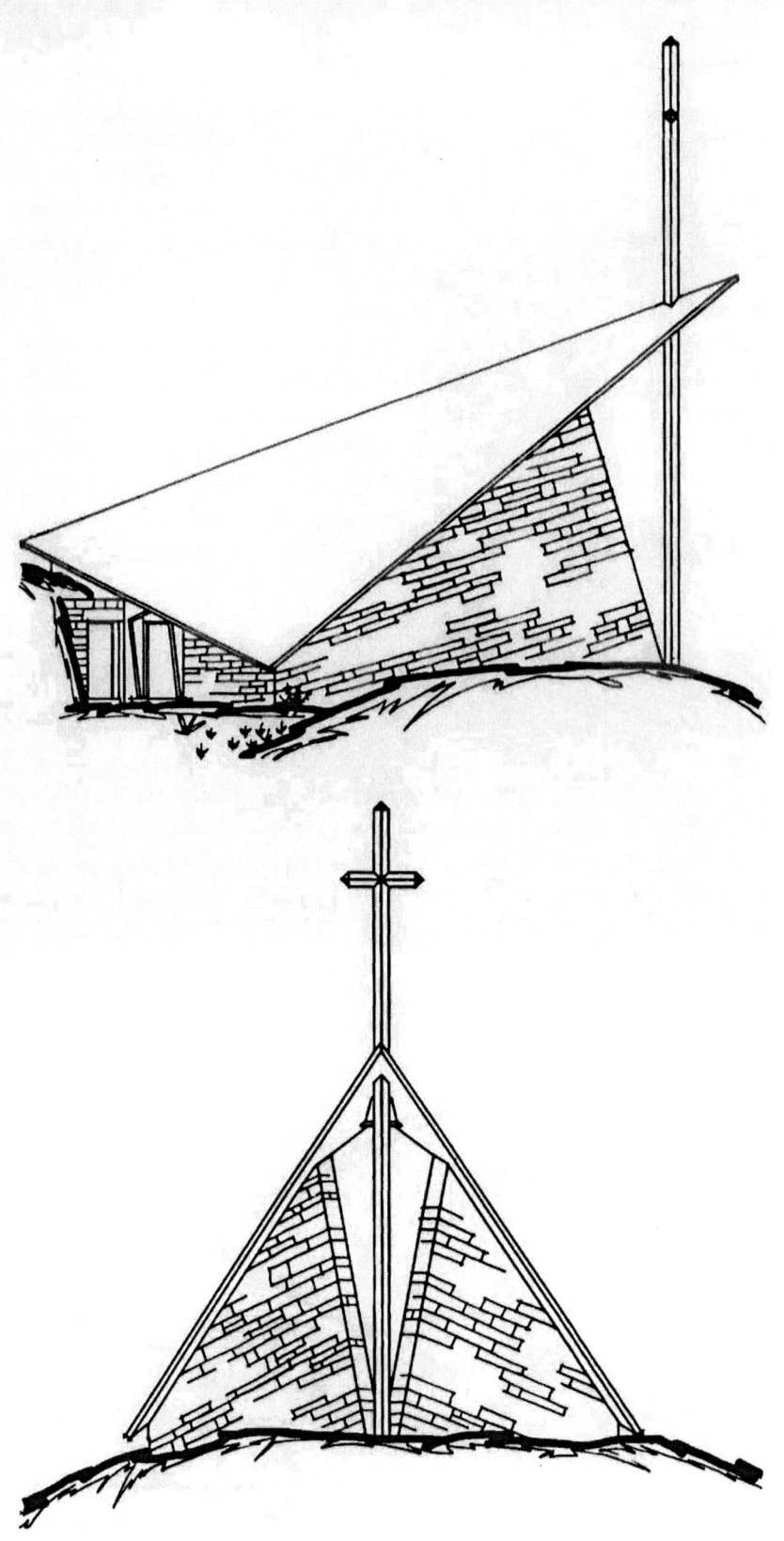

190   *Churches and Chapels*

Faced with the necessity of building on a triangular base, and limited by my scanty imagination and the desire to design something simple, humble, and sincere, I instinctively drew out a triangular elevation as well. The bow, pointing towards the deep and narrow valley, strives towards the symbol of the Cross, which rises above it, heavenwards, from whence the light must also come.

The walls were thus parted, more widely towards the top, to let in the luminous figure of our Lord, stooping gently towards the faithful.

The oblique walls, converging and rising towards the central figure, are covered by tapestry depicting the Mother and Apostles gazing towards their God. Below the window is the altar, and beyond, the splendor of nature.

Outside, as if trying to merge with the wild environment, the stones making up the walls advance in inclined rows like natural strata shaken out of the bowels of the mountain. A modest thatching roofs in this spiritual citadel.

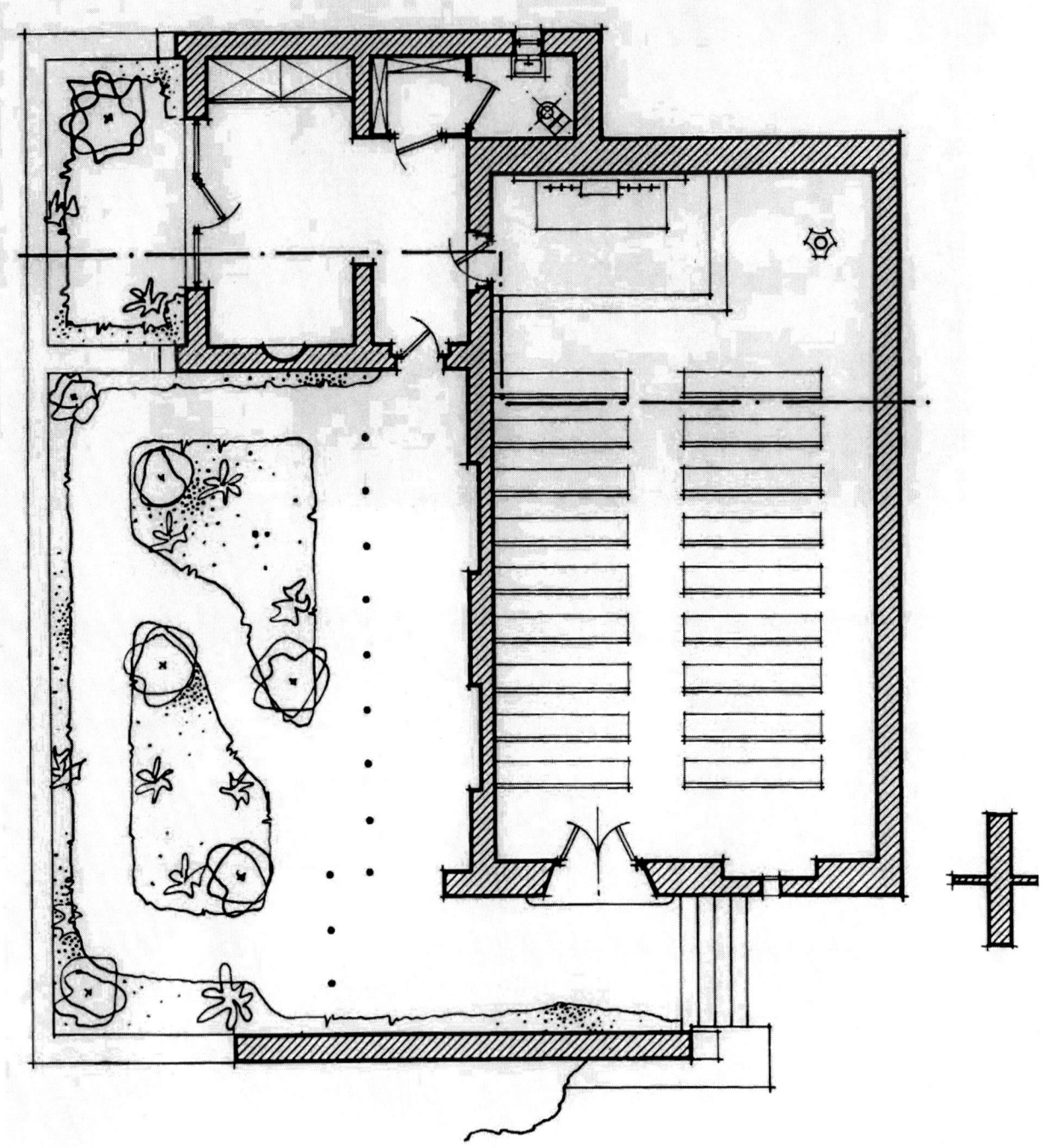

SKETCHES FOR OTHER CHAPELS

Other structural forms and ideas still await the opportunity to be translated into actual buildings. Among these are the two that illustrate these last pages.

The first structure, shown above and at left, consists of two cylindrical shells, each of them a 90-deg arc. These shells are supported by the front and rear walls alone. The skylights are placed lengthwise in the best possible position, allowing the entry not only of primary light, but also of light reflected by adjacent roof surfaces. An elevation of this building can be found on the following page.

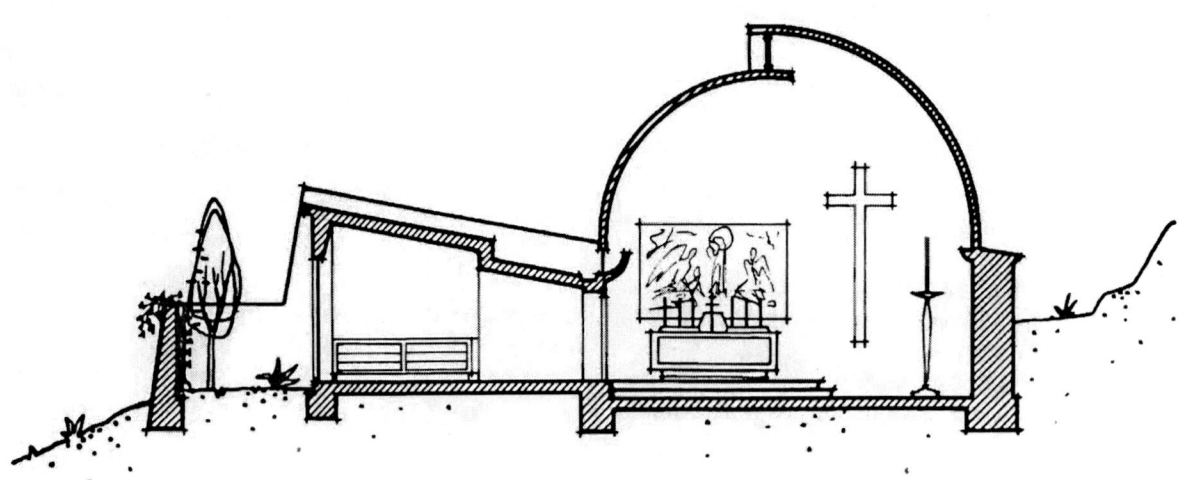

194   *Churches and Chapels*

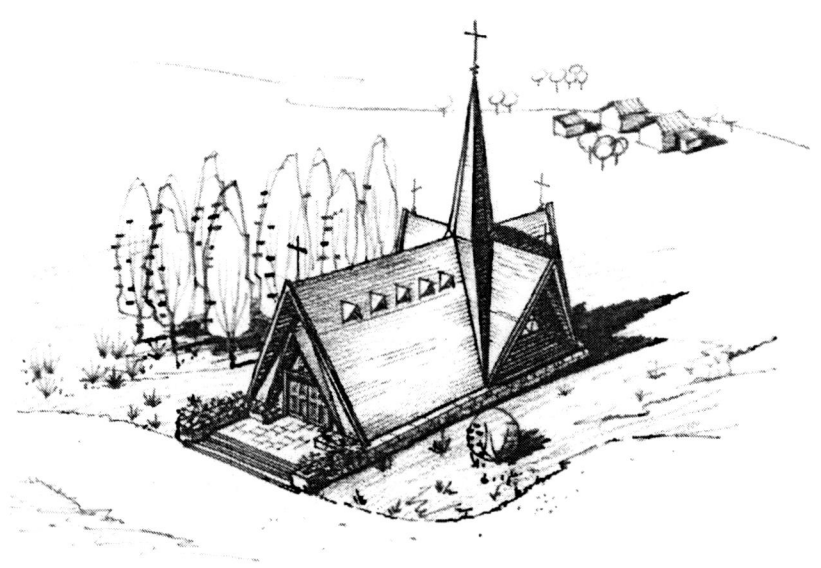

The second project yet to be realized is conceived as a timber structure, to be erected in a heavily forested region.

INDEX

CPSIA information can be obtained at www.ICGtesting.com
Printed in the USA
BVOW04s0530060915

416575BV00028B/262/P

9 781258 205423